BLESS

Stewarding our pain is a countercultural concept for many. But John Wimmer teaches us how in this read-in-a-day, live-for-a-lifetime book with gospel power and resurrection hope. *Blessed Endurance* challenges readers to redeem the despair found in life's inevitable valleys by embracing God's gifts of disciplined hope and joy.

—Harold Smith
President and CEO, *Christianity Today*

Writing with the maturity that only comes from personal experience with suffering, Wimmer does something better than play with the problem of pain; he offers a creative response for living with it.

—Peter W. Marty
Publisher, *The Christian Century*

John Wimmer speaks with the voice of a pastor who has accompanied many souls to their final earthly ritual. What makes this book exceptional is that he provides a keenly sensitive text that reflects on not only the mystery of death but also on finding hope after despair, healing after pain, and peace even during suffering.

—Mary Margaret Funk, OSB
Benedictine nun in Beech Grove, IN

Savor this beautiful and wise exploration of the anguish of human suffering and the unexpected grace of human endurance. Scriptural, mystical, practical, and deeply insightful, John Wimmer's reflections offer a sacred gift to anyone who has known suffering and yearned for meaning.

—Kerry Alys Robinson
Global Ambassador, Leadership Roundtable
Author of *Imagining Abundance: Fundraising, Philanthropy, and a Spiritual Call to Service*

Blessed Endurance provides insights from the integrity of John Wimmer's own life—a profound gift to those who want a serious discussion of the issues of pain, suffering, and hope.

—Michael J. Coyner
Bishop, The United Methodist Church (retired)

Endurance is perhaps one of the most necessary yet most overlooked virtues of the Christian life. In this honest book, John Wimmer deals directly with the inevitable pain and despair of the human condition, offering a path to hope based not on denial but on a mature, authentic relationship with the God who desires to lead us to joy—even through suffering.

—Elise Erikson Barrett
Author of *What Was Lost: A Christian Journey through Miscarriage*

What John Wimmer writes, he lives. Let John be your mentor. Listen to his words, enter into his pain, and experience God's hope.

—Adolf Hansen
Senior Scholar and Vice President Emeritus
Garrett-Evangelical Theological Seminary

This book is a companion to all who walk through suffering—a superb combination of biblical insight and theological wisdom. I have the highest respect for John Wimmer not only because of his intellect and heart but also as someone who knows what it is like to walk through the fire.

—Rob Fuquay
Senior Pastor, St. Luke's United Methodist Church, Indianapolis, IN
Author of *Which Way Lord?: Exploring Your Life's Purpose in the Journeys of Paul*

John Wimmer reminds us that we have the power to choose hope and engage in a life of blessing and meaning—regardless of our circumstances.

—Tom Albin
Director of Spiritual Formation and Congregational Life, The Upper Room

A travel guide is trustworthy only when written by someone who knows the territory; John Wimmer is such a seasoned guide. He weaves a tapestry of hope with stories culled from personal experience and framed in biblical wisdom, rich theological insight, and everyday candor. This book is a redemptive read, celebrating the strange Christian virtue of endurance and therein blessing us with strength for the journey.

—William G. Enright
Senior Pastor Emeritus, Second Presbyterian Church, Indianapolis, IN

Blessed Endurance speaks both to the mind and to the soul. I plan to share this book with my congregation and commend it to all who wrestle with the reality of suffering.

—Robert Rollins
Pastor, Murphy First United Methodist Church, Murphy, NC

Blessed ENDURANCE

MOVING BEYOND DESPAIR TO HOPE

JOHN R. WIMMER

Blessed Endurance: Moving Beyond Despair to Hope

Upper Room Books® website: books.upperroom.org

ISBN (print): 978-0-8358-1777-6 | ISBN (mobi): 978-0-8358-1778-3 | ISBN (epub): 978-0-8358-1779-0

Cover design: Bruce Gore
Interior design and typesetting: PerfecType | Nashville, TN

For Jan and David

CONTENTS

ACKNOWLEDGMENTS

The list of friends, colleagues, and family I want to thank is too long to mention each person by name. But I wish to acknowledge those who provided special guidance and support for this project.

My home congregation, St. Luke's United Methodist Church in Indianapolis, is a spiritual blessing. I am particularly grateful for the spiritual sustenance provided by Senior Pastor (and Upper Room author) Rob Fuquay, who is, in my estimation, one of the finest preachers in our nation today.

My "Mount Rushmore of father figures" have served as lifelong mentors: my father, John H. Wimmer; my father-in-law, Mark Blaising; my "doctor father," Martin Marty; and my father-in-the-faith, Adolf Hansen. My mother, Dorothy Wimmer, must also be carved on the face of this mountain just as her love is engraved on my heart.

I am thankful to Rita Collett and to the marvelous staff of Upper Room Books. I am especially thankful for my editor, Joanna Bradley, whose superb editorial skill is equal to the kindness she has shown me under difficult circumstances.

Elise Erikson Barrett helped me better understand the importance of *endurance* as an underrated Christian virtue. Because she is also such a talented friend, I am delighted her voice is the one heard on the audio version of this book.

Many colleagues and friends have gone beyond the call of duty in their help and support. They include but are not limited to the following: Lilly Endowment colleagues and friends Clay Robbins, Chris Coble, Sabina Calhoun, Jessicah Krey Duckworth, Vicki Jensen, Chanon Ross, Brian Williams, and the "Niebuhr gang" of Judy Cebula, Sara Cobb, Jackie Dowd, and Cathy Higgins. Other Endowment family members—Bill Enright, Craig Dykstra, Fred Hofheinz, Gayle Doucey, Lois Surber, and Jelaine Sparrow—have been marvelous. Dear friends and associates Kerry Robinson, Tom Locke, Matt Russell, Christine Ward, Gary and Marilyn Forbes, Mark Doucey, DJ Rise, Rick Foss, Martha and Paul Schmidt, Tim Shapiro, David Bodenhamer, David Wantz, Rebecca Arnott, Nancy Lange, Monika Nyby, Ron and Marcia Shew, Gil Rendle, the entire John Wesley Fellows community, and Parker Palmer have been blessings in myriad ways. Additionally, I am grateful to many more friends, extended family, and Lilly Endowment colleagues.

My sisters—Ann Tilton and Carol VanHoose—as well as their families have been supremely supportive in the days described in the (unexpected) epilogue and undoubtedly will continue to be so in the months to come. Sister Meg Funk, Sister Mary Luke Jones, and the entire Our Lady of Grace Benedictine community in Beech Grove, Indiana, are valued spiritual directors and prayer partners. Also, Kathleen Cahalan has been a treasured friend and spiritual guide on this journey.

Above all, my wife, Jan, and son, David, are the loves of my life. Our life together, through both triumphs and trials, is my joy. Jan's love, wisdom, and grace mean more than words can say. Her integrity, creativity, and unbounded spirit are precious gifts. David makes me proud and thankful to be his father every day. His nobility of spirit, kind heart, courage and strength in overcoming challenges, wit and humor, encyclopedic knowledge about movies old and new, and voracious quest for information about his current passions always keep me smiling and learning something new. I dedicate this book to them.

INTRODUCTION

One of the most prolific composers of Christian hymns and gospel songs was Fanny J. Crosby. Before her death in 1915, she wrote more than 8,000 hymns and songs that sold more than 100 million copies in her lifetime. She was a household name nearly a century before CNN, and she was a guest at the White House more than once. She was a pioneer in her day, transforming church and gospel music from the language and sentiments of eighteenth-century hymns into heartfelt tunes with words that better reflected the devotional spirit of most worshiping Christians of her time. Her hymns felt contemporary to people who lived more than a century ago, but we still sing many of her hymns today, including favorites such as "Pass Me Not, O Gentle Savior," "To God Be the Glory," "Jesus Is Tenderly Calling," and "Rescue the Perishing." Even newer Christian hymnals contain her gospel songs.

More astonishing than Crosby's long and remarkably productive life is that she spent almost all of it *blind*. At only six weeks old, Crosby developed an infection in her eyes that could not be treated by early-nineteenth-century medicine, so this episode left her without sight for her nearly ninety-five years. Others in the same predicament in the early 1800s may have found themselves doomed to a life of darkness and despair. But by the age of three, Crosby's deeply religious grandmother helped her memorize significant verses and even paragraphs from the Bible, and those who met her later in life were always astonished by the long biblical passages she could recite by heart. Not surprisingly, her songs are filled with heartfelt biblical phrases, themes, and imagery.

Probably Crosby's best-known hymn is "Blessed Assurance":

> Blessed assurance, Jesus is mine!
> O what a foretaste of glory divine!
> Heir of salvation, purchase of God,
> born of his Spirit, washed in his blood.
>
> This is my story, this is my song,
> praising my Savior all the day long;
> this is my story, this is my song,
> praising my Savior all the day long. (no. 369, UMH)

Through this hymn, Crosby sought to express her abiding assurance that God's redemptive work through Jesus Christ was real in her life and that the assurance of this reality was only a foretaste of the divine glory to come in the hereafter. This *assurance* that Crosby wrote about provides the basis for the story of our lives. Our *story* is not merely the recitation or retelling of the ups and downs of our personal life since birth, nor is it the unfolding of a predetermined plot like a novel or movie script. Instead, our *story* chronicles the shape of our life in *all* its dimensions—love, joy, anger, disappointment, grief, loss, triumph, defeat, illness, recovery, hope, peace, shock, victory, despair, pain, and, finally, death. In other words, Crosby's lyrics mean that our *entire story* is much bigger than a one-dimensional story. Our story is comprehensive (and, as we will see, collective), and it narrates and gives shape, meaning, and purpose to our lives. This blessed assurance—inspired by the love of God demonstrated to our world through Jesus Christ—is the basis for our *blessed endurance*.

Human life contains a mixture of experiences that includes the good and bad, ease and hardship, comfort and pain. The central question we face isn't whether we will have these ups and downs; the question is this: *How do we deal with life's inevitable ups and downs?* We may feel tempted to ask ourselves, *Who has any problem dealing with the good times?*, but the news is full of rags-to-riches stories of lottery winners who receive tens and even hundreds of millions of dollars but fall into bankruptcy and despair within a few years of winning. Why do famous and wealthy celebrities in every field—actors, athletes, musicians, and virtually any form of entertainment—face addictions, depression, overdoses, and, sometimes, suicide? Unfortunately, even the highest ups of life can be painful, and people either choose to end their lives because they can't stand it any longer or they habitually numb the pain of fame through drugs and alcohol.

The pain of life's ups and downs, left unattended, inevitably turns inward, and our internalization of this pain transforms it into a host of deeper and more troublesome feelings like anger, depression, resentment, and despair. We then tend to isolate ourselves from loved ones, friends, and those who want to help us, telling ourselves that no one wants to be around people who are angry, depressed, and resentful all the time. This sequestration and its subsequent loneliness only drive us deeper into despair. But pain has yet another trick up its sleeve: Despair and other plaguing emotions left in seclusion and unattended over time transmute yet again into physical manifestations, ranging from mild ailments to significant illnesses. Abundant medical research and experience confirm that prolonged stress and unresolved emotions (like grief) promote the opposite of wellness. Despair leads to sickness in body, mind, *and* soul.

I wrote this guidebook for those who suffer in despair (and those who help them)—and all its accompanying emotions rooted in short or prolonged experiences of pain of any kind, physical and emotional—who desire to find a spiritual pathway for *moving beyond despair to hope.* Cultivating the underrated Christian virtue of *endurance,* one of God's blessings to us if we develop the discipline to maintain it, is a cardinal requirement in making this move from pain and despair to hope and healing. But God has lovingly provided us with the tools, skills, disciplines, practices, and supportive people and communities that can help to reshape the story of our lives with a blessed assurance that blessed endurance will lead to the more abundant life God wants for us. (See John 10:10.)

Some words of warning: There are no easy answers in this book, no simple how-tos or step-by-step instructions that describe how to construct a life of hope out of despair. We will not dodge the tough questions about God, ourselves, or the tragedies of the real world we live in. Doing so only makes our problems worse rather than better.

This book is more like a travel guide or a guidebook about how to hike a long and potentially treacherous but breathtakingly beautiful trail through the wilderness. This journey is the forty-year Exodus story or the story of Jesus' forty-day stint in the wilderness, both pieces of God's Story, which provides the divine shape to creation and to our lives as Christians. So we will discuss our story as a biblical and spiritual journey in the wilderness, pausing to point out where we must watch our step and where we must halt for a moment to take in the grandeur of the glorious view God has provided. Christians of every time and place have traveled this path before us. We should allow their stories and the wisdom that they have collected both over the centuries and as recently as yesterday to guide us.

Join me on this journey that I too have traveled many, many times—sometimes kicking and screaming in protest. But that's OK. I encourage you to take this journey with others by talking to and sharing your experiences with a trusted friend, pastor, counselor, or small group. I've provided questions for individual reflection or group discussion at the end of each chapter to help gather what you are learning along the way and to allow you to go deeper into the causes of your struggle or despair, as well as to find your hope and newfound joy. May the God of everlasting hope grant you blessed endurance on your journey.

Questions for Reflection

- What attracted you to this book?
- What pain—physical, emotional, spiritual, or psychological—are you experiencing in your life?
- When you're experiencing pain, do you retreat into yourself or seek the solace of others? When you interact with people in pain, how do you respond to them?
- Remember a time when you discussed your pain with someone you trust. Journal about that experience.

1

Pain and Despair

Painful experiences—and the despair that results from them—are inevitable.

It seems silly to say something so obvious. Yet this simple statement is one of the hardest lessons we learn in life. German pastor and theologian Helmut Thielicke once described the greatest defect among American Christians in this way: "They have an inadequate view of suffering." Because we want to avoid suffering in our lives, we act as if pain doesn't hurt. Many of us try desperately to deny that pain and despair are unsavory facts of life.

Seldom do people in our society level with one another enough to admit that certain aspects of living contain pain. In childhood, we experience the growing pains associated with youthful friendships and peer pressures, dating and breaking up, schoolwork and vocational decisions. Growing into adulthood—a process that never ceases—presents struggles that are common to us all but experienced differently. For example, as some deal with the pain of childbirth, others nurse the despair of infertility. Adulthood brings its own trying passages of life, involving occupational stresses of employment or unemployment, marriage or singleness, the loss of loved ones, family issues, serious illness, midlife crises, aging parents and caregiving, accidents, retirement, and a host of other stresses provoked by everyday living.

In the face of this reality, our culture tries in countless ways to inform us as we mature from childhood into adulthood that life ought to be and remain a painless activity. From the time we are infants, our parents soothe and shield us from the discomforts of life. We are pampered with cottony-soft diapers, baby powder, and extra-gentle shampoo. In love, our parents attempt to smile away the little hurts we encounter. We are cuddled when we cry, fed when hungry, and sometimes spoiled with attention by relatives and friends who love cute babies.

Love and attention are great! Love's embrace shown to us as infants and toddlers instills within us an invaluable message: We are loved and lovable. Yet even with the best love and attention (and the most ambitious attempts at spoiling us by proud parents and gift-bearing grandparents), we cannot help but occasionally develop the measles. More painfully, some of us as children don't receive the love we need and deserve. The suffering of children is one of the most daunting examples of pain that we can experience or witness.

As we grow older, we might spend much time and money protecting ourselves, just as others sheltered us as children. We rely on aspirin to relieve our stress-induced headaches, relaxants to ease overworked muscles, and antacids to soothe full stomachs. Yet are our headaches, strained muscles, and upset stomachs the real problem or symptoms of a deeper one?

Consciously or not, we experience some pain almost daily, resulting from interactions with others. At work, home, or school, our days involve an emotional mixture of ingredients such as frustration, pressure, and competition. Beyond day-to-day discomforts, we may face severe physical and emotional disturbances. Tragedies may precipitate deeply troubling times, forcing upon us unpleasant realities we would rather avoid. Shifting economic and cultural expectations may place new pressures on engagements, marriages, parent-child relationships, living arrangements, and vocational hopes and dreams. The struggle resulting from such stress often demands that we make painful decisions, including marital or family separation, divorce, career transition, moving, or other actions that entail personal sacrifices.

Escaping Pain

Wrestling with difficult decisions, we find that living involves pain, and we are tempted to seek ways to *escape* our struggle. In extreme cases, some may try to dull the ache through the use and abuse of alcohol or drugs. After all, advertisers spend a great deal money to convince us that ridding ourselves of discomfort is simple and always desirable; we only have to buy the more powerful pain-killer that gets into our bloodstream faster or the hemorrhoid ointment that will let us sit more comfortably in our easy chair. These advertisers teach us that for a small price we can live in a painless environment.

In such a climate, if we find that our marriage involves more struggle than we anticipated, divorce or separation can seem an easy resolution to our immediate pain. In other cases, avoiding difficult marital or other family problems may be a method of evading or postponing heart-wrenching but necessary hurt. Even if we avoid these more extreme reactions to pain, we may construct imaginary walls around our inner emotional selves under the fantasy that we can be insulated from true experiences of pain. Some people even look to the church as a place where they can flee the discomfort of the "real world" by cloaking themselves within purported religious responses to pain. Yet this use of an escapist faith is no better than the use of drugs or alcohol to avoid discomfort.

Sometimes an escape into the church for shelter or sanctuary is valid; it may provide relationships and a place where we can leave behind, even if only temporarily, the trials of daily living. Or we may find an answer to a specific problem in prayer or find closer communion with God. This kind of embrace of the church in times of trouble differs greatly from escaping the world, looking for a place to hide. Faith is not an escape!

After the fleeting numbness has faded from these attempted diversions, we learn that the struggles and sore spots never really went away; along with this realization, our struggles revisit us with an even higher intensity.

So how can we view pain as part of—even essential to—the miracle of healing? One way is to remind ourselves that discomfort and despair provide excellent motivation for us to seek help from God, our church, our families and friends, medical and psychological professionals, books, or any other resource that can assist us in growth.

Embracing Pain and Despair

Given our "inadequate view of suffering," no wonder we find facing our struggles to be difficult. But before we can experience the relief and spiritual growth from the struggle that pain produces, we must first be willing to come face-to-face with our discomfort.

Two kinds of suffering exist in this world. Some people—athletes, for example—willingly take on pain for the purpose of greater strength, endurance, and improved performance. To some extent, these people enjoy pain because it clearly leads to a desired end. Others, however, do not ask for pain yet must experience it no matter how unwillingly. This kind of pain is decidedly *not* so enjoyable. We can afford to "enjoy" pain when we voluntarily assume it for physical conditioning in pursuit of sport or when we choose to take on the emotional struggle of therapy in the quest for personal fulfillment or emotional healing. When we *choose* pain or struggle, we likely realize from the beginning that sacrifices—often painful ones—must be made for the desired growth or goal to be achieved.

But what about the second kind of suffering—the type we don't choose for ourselves? Are those who do not choose their pain supposed to *enjoy* it as a coach might tell an athlete that he should "feel the burn" in training exercises or weight lifting? There are—and should be—differences in attitude and motivation between those who willingly invite disciplined discomfort into their lives with a goal in sight and those who are forced to deal with intense distress due to mistakes, accidents, illnesses, death, or the everyday relational conflicts that pile up and sometimes leave us feeling victimized by life's struggles. Although we rarely want to, if we are to *enjoy*—or, in other words, to *grow from*—the benefits available to our emotional and spiritual lives, we must first be willing to face our struggles and embrace our pain.

With the prospect of thoroughly unpleasant situations, we may think that ignoring our problems will be simpler than facing them—maybe they'll go away. Or we may try to elude the problem by numbing the hurt. But such avoidance is like sweeping dirt under the carpet; barring good luck or a miracle, the problem is still there and only temporarily out of sight. And in choosing *not* to deal with pain, we usually find that not only does the hurt refuse to go away but also the suffering tends to transfer itself into other areas of our lives.

This was the case with a man I knew named Clifford. When I first met Clifford, I did not like his sour personality; he lashed out at everyone he met. He was grumpy and short-tempered and complained constantly, bitterly describing nearly everything in his presence as "stupid." I later found out from others who knew him well that he had not always been this way. Five years before I met him, Clifford's only daughter had been killed in a car crash due to her own negligence by failing to wear a seat belt.

I remember the day Clifford first told me about his daughter's death. He began telling the story calmly, but he became progressively angrier until he finally reached a climax of rage. He thrust his face toward mine, shouting at me how *stupid* his daughter's lack of concern for her own safety was. I recognized his tone of voice. The vocal inflection he used when saying the word *stupid* about his daughter's death sounded exactly like the *stupid* he habitually applied to others. When I commented that he seemed angry about his daughter's accident (hoping this would help Clifford recognize the source of his anger so he could analyze it), he quickly got hold of himself and almost immediately returned to a fake calmness. It seemed as if nothing had happened as he concluded tersely, "I'm not angry. It doesn't matter. It's over now."

But it *wasn't* over, and it *did* matter. Clifford was angry and hurt and had not embraced those horrible feelings by admitting and recognizing their causes so that the healing process of grief might begin. How unfortunate that Clifford displayed the effects of internalized pain, despair, and anger even up to the end of his life by refusing to admit to harboring any feelings at all. Consequently, this man who so desperately needed the love and care of others to ease his pain had built a wall of repellent anger to prevent others who might offer their concern from getting close to him.

The key to embracing pain is to be honest about what is hurting us, but we cannot always easily identify the sources of our despair. Of course, when we experience a tragedy like the death of a loved one, we know the source of our grief. Even so, sometimes we disguise our hurts through avoidance techniques and coping mechanisms we have cultivated over the years. Maybe we are too detached or too scared to do the demanding work of embracing pain—for contrary to what some believe, dealing with emotions is hard work. Emotional work like this, in fact, is more draining than physical labor. Or it could be that we are afraid of other hurts that we may lay bare if we honestly confront the sources our distress. Often, when we are honest with our feelings, we find clusters of other strong feelings accompanying our despair, such as anger, guilt, rage, sadness, insecurity, disappointment, loneliness, confusion—the list is long. When we undergo rigorous self-examination, we suddenly may find ourselves struggling with many more questions than we had anticipated. We may even feel bogged down by analyzing and working through these many-faceted feelings—a sensation I've heard called *paralysis by analysis*.

Still, we must embrace these feelings no matter how challenging.

Alone with Pain and Despair

During the early stages of honest recognition of our pain and despair (in which we will likely identify other emotions and struggles), we may feel alone, hurt, or misunderstood; we may even consider giving up altogether. We tell ourselves that no one really cares or understands. Sometimes even God seems distant!

At stressful times like these, we can remind ourselves that other persons of great personal faith have felt the same way. Many of the psalms give us insight into feelings of loneliness and bitterness as the psalmists embrace and wrestle with despair. In fact, an entire group called the lament psalms reveals the psalmists' struggles to understand their own suffering as they too ask, "Where are you, God?" Here are some examples:

How long, O LORD? Will you forget me forever?
How long will you hide your face from me?
How long must I bear pain in my soul,
and have sorrow in my heart all day long?
How long shall my enemy be exalted over me? (Ps. 13:1-2)

My wounds grow foul and fester
because of my foolishness;
I am utterly bowed down and prostrate;
all day long I go around mourning. . . .
I am utterly spent and crushed;

I groan because of the tumult of my heart.
(Ps. 38:5-6, 8)

I say to God, my rock,
"Why have you forgotten me?
Why must I walk about mournfully
because the enemy oppresses me?"
As with a deadly wound in my body,
my adversaries taunt me,
while they say to me continually,
"Where is your God?" (Ps. 42:9-10)

Although the Bible often offers us inspiration and comfort, it also gives us a glimpse into the of loneliness and suffering of others. The Bible contains many examples of great figures of faith expressing their feelings of dissatisfaction with pain and suffering and confessing how they feel alone in despair. But none of these examples is more powerful than Jesus' words on the cross.

Despair and the Cross

No matter who we are or how much faith we have, when we face or embrace pain and despair, we likely will cry out to God like the psalmist does in Psalm 42: "Why have you forgotten me?" (v. 9). When our faith in God plays an important role in our life, we naturally will trust God enough to cry out in our anguish—no matter how uncomfortable we feel in questioning or being angry at God. Many believe that questioning is contrary to faith; yet honest questioning is probably one of the most positive expressions of faithfulness and trust in God. Doubt and agonizing questions can only exist where we find profound love and respect—and God loves us and respects us enough to allow, and even welcome, our doubts and questions.

The greatest comfort and example available to us in our lonely, desert-like places of despair is remembering that Jesus himself felt the excruciating pain and despair of the cross. In fact, the word *excruciating* comes from the Latin word meaning "to crucify." For in his greatest moment of agony and despair, loneliness and abandonment, Jesus cries out words taken from a lament psalm: "My God, my God, why have you forsaken me?" (Matt. 27:46, quoting Ps. 22:1).

From Jesus on the cross and the words he spoke there, we can learn much about God's presence amid the suffering of the world and our own pain. For nothing shows us more clearly that suffering, pain, and despair are a part of life to be embraced than the way Jesus faces the sorrow he knows to be inevitable as he makes his way to Jerusalem. He too feels tempted to avoid or escape the struggle. On the night before Jesus' crucifixion, just after the Last Supper, Jesus withdraws to the garden of Gethsemane. The Gospel of Matthew tells us the following: "[Jesus] said to his disciples, 'Sit here while I go over there and pray.' He took with him Peter and the two sons of Zebedee, and began to be grieved and agitated. Then he said to them, 'I am deeply grieved, even to death; remain here, and stay awake with me'" (26:36-38). The Gospel of Matthew describes

Jesus as "agitated" and "grieved, even to death"; in other words, Jesus was nearly in panic. In this state of mind, a profoundly distressed Jesus goes off by himself and makes a human and vulnerable request of God: "My Father, if it is possible, let this cup pass from me" (Matt. 26:39). Even Jesus wants to avoid the suffering of the cross.

Who among us has been more painfully honest with God about our desire to avoid pain and suffering? Who has prayed more earnestly for God to take away the difficulty we face or that is immediately before us? Why do we imagine or think of Jesus as so far above our own humanity to believe that he does not despair or seek to avoid pain or plead with God to "let this cup pass"? This would deny the humanity of Jesus. No, this critical moment in his life was placed in the Bible to show Christians that the vulnerability and humanity we see in God's beloved Son is precisely the same as our own human vulnerability.

Jesus does not want to suffer the pain, but after he pleads with God for the cup to pass from him, he continues by saying, "Yet not what I want but what you want" (Matt. 26:39). Of course, Jesus then suffers an agonizing, humiliating death. He is abandoned, in despair, grieved, worried to death, and human. But he is also faithful, sacrificial, forgiving, and divine. Human *and* divine. This paradoxical combination is what makes Jesus our Lord. He is God made flesh so that humanity can see, experience, and understand the love, grace, and mercy of God in the only form through which our limited humanity can perceive the Divine.

The Paradox of Spiritual Growth

In some sense, we never will understand nor fully explain why our lives must contain pain and despair. No matter how earnest our prayers, no matter how penetrating or intelligent our questions, we will not ever thoroughly know why. But we live surrounded by God-made paradoxes—statements or beliefs that seem contradictory or in opposition to common sense but are still true. We know that in the spring, the delicate shoots of flowers will break through the soil left hard from the winter's snow and ice. We know that a tiny planted seed, if nurtured to maturity, will yield grain—but it had to be sacrificed to the ground first. We know that a pruned fruit tree will bear more and larger fruit than one left wild to grow unattended. And we know that our scrapes and cuts and bruises—as well as most of our minor and major surgeries—usually will enter the miraculous process of healing. We have witnessed these God-created processes whereby hurt leads to healing, practice to proficiency, and despair to hope.

Jesus' own life and death offer a paradox through which God reveals God's own self in a sacrificial life, a despairing death, and a hopeful resurrection to show us how we may grow spiritually. And yet, this question may continue to plague us: Is God responsible for creating or allowing suffering to be part of our world? This question has never been answered with satisfactory results after centuries of debate, but it is part of the paradox. In this debate, we find a hidden kernel of truth that we can join hands with a great cloud of witnesses and be certain that God remains present throughout our suffering and pain, nurturing us and giving spiritual growth to all who move from despair to hope.

Hope is the lifeline tossed out to us from God. It sustains us when we feel like we are drowning, and God gently pulls us and the lifeline toward the shores of spiritual growth. With hope, we also have faith—not faith that we will be spared pain and despair but faith in the God who will lead us through the difficult times. Therefore, in our struggle to understand God's will, let us not concentrate solely on our pain and despair (although we know we are to accept them); instead, let us look with hope and faith toward attaining new, rich experiences of the abundant life God has given us.

Questions for Reflection

- Explain the difference between challenges you have chosen to take on and those you did not choose. How were you able to embrace the pain of the former? How did you react to the pain of the latter?
- What difficult experience have you endured? What spiritual and emotional insights did you gain?
- What lessons do you take away from the lament psalms about expressing your honest feelings to God?
- God understands suffering through God's own experience of hopelessness and death on the cross. What have you learned about God's willingness to suffer with you?

2

Moving toward Spiritual Growth

We have seen that asking God, "Why am I suffering?" is a healthy response to pain and despair, but we have also noted that expecting God's deliverance from travail may not be fruitful. Unrelenting questioning can plague us and divert our attention from where it needs to be placed: on seeking spiritual growth. Even as we embrace our pain and despair, we must also guard against allowing these feelings to get the best of us—which may happen if we concentrate on what seems to be the futility of our spiritual battle. We should exercise our God-given ability to respond in faith instead of allowing a painful situation to control us. As opposed to intensifying the hurt by calling undue amounts of attention to it, we must work toward focusing our attention on our *response* to pain and despair—and begin to realize that spiritual growth will result from our response.

The writer of Hebrews, having summarized the faith of great leaders and the Hebrew scriptures, admonishes us to concentrate on a faithful response to suffering rather than clinging to that which holds us back:

> Therefore, since we are surrounded by so great a cloud of witnesses, let us also lay aside every weight and the sin that clings so closely, and let us run with perseverance the race that is set before us, looking to Jesus the pioneer and perfecter of our faith, who for the sake of the joy that was set before him endured the cross, disregarding its shame, and has taken his seat at the right hand of the throne of God. . . . Endure trials for the sake of discipline. God is treating you as children; for what child is there whom a parent does not discipline? If you do not have that discipline in which all children share, then you are illegitimate and not his children. Moreover, we had human parents to discipline us, and we respected them. Should we not be even more willing to be subject to the Father of spirits and live? For they disciplined us for a short time as seemed best to them, but he disciplines us for our good, in order that we may share his holiness. (12:1-2, 7-10)

And then the most important verse:

> Now, discipline always seems painful rather than pleasant at the time, but later it yields the peaceful

> fruit of righteousness to those who have been trained by it. (Heb. 12:11)

The image of the heavenly parent used in this passage may evoke recollections of the earthly parent who dragged us by the ear to sit in time-out. We all have heard a loving parent utter on such occasions, "This is going to hurt me more than it hurts you!" Few of us believe this parental cliché when we are children, but if we become parents, our attitude becomes strangely different. To parents who must help their children learn difficult, even painful lessons, these words about discipline suddenly speak truth.

The original Greek word translated as *discipline* in the Hebrews passage is derived from the same root word as "to instruct" and "to learn." Therefore, the *discipline* mentioned in this passage is not necessarily to be associated with punishment (although the element of punishment is indeed present in the passage). Rather than regarding discipline as punitive, this portion of scripture emphasizes discipline as learning, as a deepening spiritual experience of growing more Christlike. In other words, Hebrews tells us that when we are in the midst of pain, suffering, or despair, we should view the discipline required there as an opportunity for spiritual growth rather than regard it as castigation by an angry, capricious parental figure. Although this discipline is difficult and often painful, the suffering that comes from discipline yields a peaceful righteousness from God.

Fire-Refined Faith

The epistle of First Peter was written when persecution of the early Christians by the Roman State was rampant. Citizenship in the Empire demanded full allegiance, meaning loyalty to Christian beliefs undermined imperial rule. Christians who refused to bow to the throne and worship the Caesars as gods (as was often practiced) were sometimes severely persecuted and, ultimately, executed.

First Peter begins by addressing Christians who are undergoing such persecution:

> Blessed be the God and Father of our Lord Jesus Christ! By his great mercy he has given us a new birth into a living hope through the resurrection of Jesus Christ from the dead, and into an inheritance that is imperishable, undefiled, and unfading, kept in heaven for you, who are being protected by the power of God through faith for a salvation ready to be revealed in the last time. In this you rejoice, even if now for a little while you have had to suffer various trials, so that the genuineness of your faith—being more precious than gold that, though perishable, is tested by fire—may be found to result in praise and glory and honor when Jesus Christ is revealed. (1:3-7)

We are imperfect humans in need of "refinement" like a precious metal that requires purification by fire, which is to say we need to be purged of impurities in our faith. First

Peter compares this purification to the "testing" of gold, which is accomplished only by the burnishing of the refiner's fire. We observe in this passage, however, that the opening admonition of First Peter was intended as an encouraging reminder to the persecuted not to look at the immediate pain of their fiery testing but to cultivate the vision to see beyond the "various trials" they currently face in order to glimpse life "born anew" as a result of their faithfulness and endurance. The letter continues in this way:

> Now that you have purified your souls by your obedience to the truth so that you have genuine mutual love, love one another deeply from the heart. You have been born anew, not of perishable but of imperishable seed, through the living and enduring word of God. For
>
> "All flesh is like grass
>   and all its glory like the flower of grass.
> The grass withers,
>   and the flower falls,
> but the word of the Lord endures forever."
>
> That word is the good news that was announced to you. (1 Pet. 1:22-25)

The metaphor of suffering as fire reflects how we feel when we embrace travail, struggle, and despair. Fire burns and it hurts! Cauterization by hot iron taken directly from a fire was one of the earliest medical remedies to burn and thereby purify injured flesh to halt infection so that healing could begin. Barbaric to us; effective treatment before antibiotics. Refining fire also purifies and strengthens, forging toughness and durability in precious metals. Like gold, which can be molded into artwork of immortal beauty when properly refined, purified, and melted, faith that is refined through the furnace of disciplined faithfulness—discipleship—can be molded after the immortal image of God in Christ.

From the "refiner's fire," impurities in our faith surface in our consciousness. And having recognized these impurities, we can no longer be satisfied by allowing them to remain in our soul. For once we have been tempered by the fiery discipline and learning of dealing with our pain and despair, we can no longer be as self-centered in our relationships with others or as insensitive to their trials as we may have been before our own purification. Or we may grow spiritually by learning that we do not trust God as much as we thought and thereby need to learn how to live out our faith in God truly. Or we may learn patience simply by having to practice it as we search for the emotional or spiritual roots of our despair, as we wait for healing, as we hope for broken relationships to mend, or as we realize that some relationships are toxic to us and we must sever those ties. In all these areas (and many more), the imperfections of our faith and Christian life become known to us through the refiner's fire so that we may begin to purify ourselves spiritually by the grace of God.

Maturing, Enduring Faith

> My brothers and sisters, whenever you face trials of any kind, consider it nothing but joy, because you know that the testing of your faith produces *endurance*; and let endurance have its full effect, so that you may be mature and complete, lacking in nothing.
>
> —James 1:2-4 (emphasis added)

For centuries, suffering has been likened to groping in the darkness, shivering out in the cold, or being stranded in the desert. Drawing from these rich resources in his book *A Cry of Absence: Reflections for the Winter of the Heart,* Martin E. Marty corresponds the passing seasons of the year to the seasons of spiritual life. When someone close to us dies or we experience some other kind of loss, our spirituality may have a cold, wintry feeling (as opposed to a warm, summery feeling when things seem to be going well). Marty notes that many people who claim to be "spirit-filled" never embrace or even recognize this type of wintry spirituality because they think it to be "un-Christian" to let on that their life isn't going well. Marty describes the stance of this "spirit-filled" person toward life's challenges: "Never does the storm of a troubled heart receive its chance to be heard. The Lord has satisfied every need, one hears, so it would be a sin to stare once more at the void within. Christ is the answer, the spirit is warm and no chill is ever allowed between the boards or around the windows of the soul."[1]

As Marty suggests, many people view denial of suffering as the most faithful way to respond to it in a so-called "Christian" manner. Truthfully, such a response expresses *immature* faith. It presumes that all suffering is inherently evil and that the visitation of travail in our lives is something to be denied rather than heeded. Failing to cultivate this fruitful ground for spiritual growth is to miss a deeply rewarding experience in Christian life. Although denial is a necessary coping mechanism embedded within our emotions for dealing with the shock of death, sudden tragedies, or illness, *extended* denial blocks spiritual and emotional growth. Denial blunts growing in the faith because it short-circuits the discipline (learning) required to become a better Christian.

In James's epistle, we read, "consider it nothing but joy" whenever we face trials of any kind. In the previous section, we read the following from First Peter: "In this you rejoice, even if now for a little while you have had to suffer various trials." Is the mature spiritual impulse to rejoice when we are in travail?

The words *joy* and *rejoice* as they appear in James and First Peter do not mean what they seem first glance. The rejoicing we find here is not a shallow, syrupy, or optimistic refusal to admit that problems exist; instead, it is the realistic recognition of struggle bolstered by the decision to rejoice in knowing that God is working to bring us through strife to greater spiritual depth. Yes, it may be tough if not impossible to rejoice when suffering, but such joy will not take the form of emotional jubilance or elation. James proclaims that suffering may be considered as joy when the encounter produces the spiritual virtue of *steadfastness*. And steadfastness, when allowed to flower into fullness, produces the most attractive bloom of all qualities: Christian maturity. Authentic Christian maturity, then, is a steadfastness that we attain not by denial. It is a quality that, like any other kind of maturity, accrues with age, hard work, and a lot of bruising experience. It is the ability to redirect our thoughts beyond immediate woes in order to realize the spiritual growth that results from tests of faith.

Only in this sense can we truly rejoice when we meet various trials. No one *enjoys* this kind of joy, but with trials come a more mature faith that is enriched by meaningful insights and the spiritual treasure that awaits us when we grapple with the difficulties we face. Thus, opportunities to grow closer to God, gain in spiritual wisdom, and grow in Christian steadfastness are worth rejoicing.

Finding Meaning in Our Trials

In biblical times—and even today—people blamed physical infirmities, diseases, mental illnesses, disabilities, and even troublesome personal traits on a person's own sins or on the "sins of the fathers"—a person's parents. (See Ezekiel 18:20; Exodus 20:5.) We now know through modern medical research that some physical and mental difficulties are hereditary (such as hemophilia, cystic fibrosis, and depression) and that certain psychological troubles can be traced back at least in part to parental issues. However,

Jesus reiterates to his disciples that physical and mental illnesses as well as disabilities are *not* a punishment for some long-forgotten misdemeanor committed by a person's mother or father. On one such occasion in the Gospel of John, Jesus encounters a blind man:

> As [Jesus] walked along, he saw a man blind from birth. His disciples asked him, "Rabbi, who sinned, this man or his parents, that he was born blind?" Jesus answered, "Neither this man nor his parents sinned; he was born blind so that God's works might be revealed in him." (9:1-3)

Earlier, when we examined the passage from Hebrews, we spoke of seeing our difficulties as God's way of disciplining us—that is, teaching us as a parent instructs a child. But Jesus' words to his disciples concerning the blind man give us a clearer understanding of spiritual growth that results from discipline (learning): The work of God may be displayed through the spiritual growth inextricably bound to our physical and/or mental challenges.

I learned this lesson in a relatively modest way when I severely broke my right wrist a few years ago. Since I am right-handed, this break led to many unforeseen challenges. My wrist was placed in a cast for a month, and I underwent surgery to secure a metal plate and screws in my wrist. After another month in a cast, months of physical therapy, and a year of work regaining the use of my hand and fingers, I learned the painful lesson of my dependency on my right hand. I could only use a computer awkwardly, typing slowly by pecking out letters with two or three of my left fingers. My handwriting was worse than a doctor's prescription. Buttoning and zipping clothes, washing my hands, blowing my nose, tying my shoes, knotting my tie, reaching for things in pockets—and thousands of other daily tasks small and large—each became a daunting new chore as I struggled to relearn preschool-level motor skills. I felt like a helpless child.

Over time, however, after months of frustration and necessary repetition, I got better and better at using my left hand alone. I discovered how to align and use the zipper on my coat or button my clothes with only one hand. I figured out how to knot my tie and tie my shoes only with my left hand. I even learned to write left-handed, though I wouldn't get high marks for penmanship. I learned to do so many things—or to compensate for them—that they are too numerous to list. As my wise grandmother used to say, "Those who refuse to learn new tricks become old dogs!"

Physical and/or mental disabilities and challenges teach lessons. Beyond the skills I learned to accomplish left-handed, my outlook on the world and others also changed. I can never look at an amputee the same way again. My admiration for anyone with a missing limb is enormous. All people with handicaps or disabilities who must navigate our society and its inaccessible or inhospitable institutions, buildings, and systems—not to mention thoughtless and intolerant people—exhibit a grit and can-do spirit that is a combination of determination, character, flexibility, and nerve. These are all human, moral, and spiritual virtues. In almost every person I know who lives with a disability or handicap, I see God's hand at work, helping my brothers or sisters (and their family, friends, and loved ones) grow and mature.

Does God send these challenges to people so that they may develop these traits and skills? In a culture where this idea is commonplace, Jesus proclaims the cruelty and injustice of such a belief. God did not cause my broken wrist to teach me a lesson, nor does God inflict the burdens of disability or infirmity on people due to their own sins or those of their parents.

Of course, in this story, Jesus heals the man of his blindness, and presumably the healing of his disability manifested the work of God. Many who hurt desperately pray to God, asking for a miracle. And too many charlatan "Christian" ministers have made a comfortable living peddling such false "miraculous healing." Although much mystery and controversy surrounds this issue, many faithful people believe they have indeed been miraculously healed of physical and mental ills—and I believe many of them have. All healing is a miracle, the gift of a gracious God. But many other equally faithful people have also diligently prayed for miracles but do not find themselves healed of their diseases—and I believe that the absence of a miracle had nothing to do with the supplicant's amount of faith. Do some people happen to know the magic formula that gives God permission to produce miracles, while others continue to suffer only because of their ignorance of this divine incantation? Some believe that with enough faith any miracle can happen; others who pray for a miracle will later stand at a graveside, wondering if their lack of faith prohibited a miracle.

No one fully understands the mystery of healing or health. And Jesus most certainly does not perform miracles just to prove that God possesses the power to heal "on demand" based on capricious criteria. Rather, the story about Jesus' encounter with the blind man—and many other stories of healing in the Bible—invites us to broaden our perception of the healing, wholeness, and spiritual growth that God provides to all who pray for miracles.

Above all, I believe the *spiritual meaning* we accrue by moving from despair to hope ought to be the chief criterion by which we perceive and receive healing, rather than the eradication of disease from our minds and bodies. For example, perhaps one party in a troubled marriage is terminally ill, but the relationship may be reconciled in the meaningful period of time leading to death. A couple dealing with the hurt of infertility may find comfort in accepting that their situation in no way lessens their capacity to love an adopted child. A person with an addiction may feel helpless in battling it alone but attests to the power of healing through belonging to a 12-step group or community that offers support and accountability. Some people who live with clinical depression are the most compassionate, empathetic, and effective listening healers I know. Other types of healing may result from dealing with suffering—healing that we have neither the capacity to imagine nor the perceptiveness to observe.

I once conducted the funeral of a dear friend named Grace. Only a few years before her death, she lost her husband of over fifty years. Only weeks after his burial, she learned that a malignancy had been raging through her body undetected. Through magnificent perseverance, while grieving the loss of her husband, Grace underwent agonizing chemotherapy treatments, hoping they would arrest the disease. The treatments failed, but Grace never gave up hope that one day she would be rid of her cancer.

Grace's health continued to deteriorate, and following a long and valiant struggle, she died. As the one who would deliver her eulogy, I was tormented over what to say about the last months of Grace's life, which were full of grief and suffering. She was a saintly person, so no one would have thought to blame her for these misfortunes. And I confess I was tempted by questions of why such a marvelous woman had died a lingering and painful death. Why wasn't *she* healed? If faith and hope were the keys to unlocking the door to healing, Grace certainly possessed them in abundance.

But then I began to recall Grace's last months and the many people who came into contact with her. Friends stopped by or phoned to say hello and encourage her; family members surrounded Grace with their love during those last days. Because Grace was the kind of person who had always cared for others in need, grateful church members prepared and delivered food to her visiting family, handled errands, did the laundry, sent cards, and lifted her in prayer. To these people, Grace's words and actions were always kind and, well, *graceful*. Even though she couldn't hide the pain she was in, Grace never lost hope that healing would come—and her hope lived on even after her death. At Grace's funeral, I heard people say, "This horrible disease may have conquered the body, but *nothing* defeated her spirit, her faith, or her *hope*!" Her ultimate hope had always been to be with God in heaven. I feel certain that Grace's hope was completely fulfilled by dwelling in God's eternal presence.

As we correlate Grace's struggle to be healed with the idea of the *meaning* found in suffering (rather than in physical healing), I cannot help but feel that the witness of Grace's death and her tenacious grip on hope proved to be the manifestation of God's healing power. The people who came to visit Grace did not walk away grumbling why God had not healed her. They left her presence inspired and aware that in her spiritual maturity, strength, and endurance, they had witnessed a rare display of hope and faith in God. Grace's disease was not contagious, but her hope was. Through her life and death, many people began a healing process by witnessing a new possibility of deeper spiritual meaning for their own lives. God's power is on display in the *meaning* we find in our pain, suffering, and despair. This is no less a miracle than miraculous healing.

God Works for Good, In Everything

If God does not necessarily punish us for misconduct, as we have learned in the story of Jesus and the blind man,

God also does not necessarily reward us with good things in this life because we have been faithful. In the Christian faith, we affirm God's love and care for all people equally, no matter how good or bad they are or have been.

Certainly, some biblical stories describe characters that benefitted materially from following God's demands or guidance, often despite their immorality. But it has long been part of the Christian tradition—as well as the result of closely examining the Bible about this matter and not just particular stories in isolation—that God does not dispense rewards for good deeds as if handing out treats to an obedient pet.

Because God cares for us like an earthly parent, God also wants the best for us. We often have a difficult time understanding how God's will operates, just as children do not grasp why their parents scold them to stay away from a hot stove. Especially when we are struggling or suffering, we may feel God's will is nowhere to be found. Yet we read this line in Paul's letter to the Romans: "We know that all things work together for good for those who love God, who are called according to his purpose" (8:28) or "We know that in all things God works for the good of those who love him, who have been called according to his purpose" (8:28, NIV).

Does Romans 8:28 mean that everything that happens to us is God's will, as this verse seems to suggest? Or that everything always works out the way we want it to if we only love God enough? Does it mean that God has a predetermined and inflexible plan for our lives that will naturally unfold no matter what? Does it suggest that if bad things happen to us—or when we experience travail and despair—that these afflictions are inflicted upon us by God for some unfathomable divine purpose? Any of these implications suggested from Romans 8:28 is troubling to me.

I am grateful to my mentor and friend Adolf Hansen for helping me understand the true meaning of this important verse. Besides being a mentor and friend, Dr. Hansen is a respected biblical scholar and writer. Because of his highly specialized knowledge of the Greek language and the New Testament, Dr. Hansen has written that rather than "all things work together for good for those who love God," a *better* and *more accurate* translation of the Greek sentence structure Paul used is this: "God works for good, in everything."[2] In other words, *God* is the subject of the sentence—not *everything works together*.

The notion that everything that happens to us is God's will and that God's will is good only *if* we love God is very different from the idea that God intends to be at work for our good in everything. The former implies that everything that happens to us is a matter of God's will and purpose, so when things don't go our way, we must figure out what God's hidden will is and how we missed it or discern how we have not loved God enough to merit the favor of God's goodness. Dr. Hansen's translation states that God actively works in the midst of everything that happens to us, good or bad—not that everything will turn out the way we want but that God is at work no matter what we face in order to bring about good in our lives. So God is not passive in the face of everything that happens to us, for God constantly "works for good." But God's care is not dependent on our devotional state or measured by our love of God; instead, God's active "work for good" is an ever-present expression of God's love and goodness. *In everything!*

Dr. Hansen's small change in the biblical translation more accurately reflects what the apostle Paul was trying to communicate to the church in Rome about God's will, and Dr. Hansen's English version of Romans 8:28 has much to suggest about the way God's will works *actively* in our lives, especially when we are questioning God in times of trouble. It also steers us clear of potential spiritual and emotional harm that grows out of commonly held but dangerously false ideas about how God "controls" all things in our lives, a belief that inappropriate interpretations of this passage can reinforce. God does not dole out good or ill by taking our spiritual temperature.

Years ago, as my college professor in a theology class, Dr. Hansen also taught me about the human understanding of God's will as related in the classic book by Leslie D. Weatherhead, *The Will of God.*[3] In this book, Weatherhead distinguishes God's will into three categories: the *intentional,* the *circumstantial,* and the *ultimate.* Each is the will of God—but each type of will manifests itself differently according to changing circumstances in the course of our lives.

Weatherhead's book began as a series of sermons originally prepared for members of his congregation, City Temple in London, who were suffering the personal hardships and tragic consequences of World War II. The City

Temple building itself had been destroyed by bombing. In the shadow of their church building in rubble and to parishioners whose lives were often in shambles as they lived in fear and uncertainty, Weatherhead preached that in such situations we use the words *the will of God* much too cavalierly. We confuse ourselves by not understanding the many ways in which God's will is expressed and how that will works in the ever-shifting mazes of our intertwining lives. At that time, God's people lived surrounded by destroyed homes, businesses, and churches; people were killed by the randomness of falling bombs in war. Too many in our world still live in such terror.

Weatherhead notes that we often think of God's will as a narrow path down which we must dutifully tread. And if we choose a wrong fork in the road, we consign ourselves irreparably to the hazards of a life other than the one that God *intended* for us. In this way of understanding God's will, we easily elevate any troubles or difficulties we encounter in life—not to mention experiences like war, natural disaster, or injurious accidents—and attribute them to some false move we made or to a seemingly unforgiveable sin we committed that took us off God's intended but hidden path. One wrong choice away from God's will, we can thus believe, is the source of our troubles.

The result, from this point of view, is often that we scour our past to figure out exactly where and in what way we went wrong. Confusion and even spiritual harm then prevail when we attribute one aspect of God's will to all situations in our lives. This viewpoint means we generally think *God's will* is chiefly and naturally *God's intention.* But we also believe God loves us. So how can God both love us and *intend* for bad things to happen to us, especially when we have tried to be good people and to follow God's will? I heard this confusion in the voice of a widow at her husband's funeral who explained to me that she must accept the fact that he had been "taken" from her, clearly implying that God did the taking through death. Even though these words came out of her mouth, her face and spirit cried out, "If God loves me, why would God take my husband away from me?" I saw the same confusion in a friend and devoted church member who when his musically talented daughter committed suicide seemed to gain strange comfort by telling visitors attending the funeral, "God must have needed another soprano in the heavenly choir." What kind of God would take away a parent's beloved and talented daughter by causing a teenager to take her own life simply to fill in the four-part harmony of a choir singing God's praises? This would not be a God worthy of worship, and these examples show false perceptions of God's intentional will.

In the Gospel of Matthew, we find Jesus' parable about the lost sheep. Jesus concludes the parable by saying, "It is not the will of your Father in heaven that one of these little ones should be lost [or "perish," NIV]" (Matt. 18:14). From this scripture and many others, we may assume that it is *not* God's *intention* for little ones (or, presumably, any of the rest of God's children) to be lost, to suffer, or to perish. Yet why do we continue to believe that when bad things happen to us they somehow must be God's *will*? One partial (though still inadequate) answer is that because humans are free to serve and follow God, we are also free to choose what is sinful or evil. And some of the sinful choices we make do indeed lead to suffering for ourselves and others.

Yet, according to Weatherhead, even within the evil and sinful circumstances brought about through exercising the freedom God bestows upon us as human beings, God still wills us to choose what is worthy rather than that which would cause or propagate evil and suffering. So even in the worst circumstances, when we have made terrible choices that have caused us and others to experience profound distress, God maintains what Weatherhead calls a *circumstantial will* for us—a type of God's will that may be a bit or even entirely different from God's *intentional will*, which was God's original loving intention for us *before circumstances changed*.

God's circumstantial will may then be different from God's intention. God did not intend for a teenage soprano to commit suicide to fill an empty spot of the heavenly chorus. No one was more aggrieved than God by this act! Yet even in situations that arise in life that God certainly does not intend, God's *circumstantial will* remains active and working for good—always.

This fresh biblical insight changes the way we think about what happens to us in relation to God's will. Situations in our lives are not always what God intends or intended. But this does not lessen God's power to work for good in all life's circumstances. This idea about God's circumstantial will may comfort us because it does not place difficulties we sometimes face at odds with God's intentional will. In fact, our trials, pain, and despair may be contrary to what God intends. But God loves us enough to give us freedom, which we use for both the good and the bad, and to give all of creation freedom to transform life-giving rain into life-threatening tornados, hurricanes, and other natural disasters that we mislabel "acts of God."

Instead, God's circumstantial will is as lovingly pliable as necessary to remain actively at work for our good, no matter the situations in which we find ourselves. God's circumstantial will, contrary to dishonoring God's sovereignty and power, raises them to even higher levels because God's love is large enough to transcend any situation and to roll with the punches when we brawl with life. As Paul reminds us in Romans, "I am convinced that neither death, nor life, nor angels, nor rulers, nor things present, nor things to come, nor powers, nor height, nor depth, nor anything else in all creation, will be able to separate us from the love of God in Christ Jesus our Lord" (8:38-39). This is good news—and the news gets even better! Even though God allows God's own original intentional will to be thwarted or delayed through circumstances brought about by our God-granted freedom (in order that we as humans may freely choose to love and follow God or not), God above all maintains an *ultimate will* that cannot be thwarted by our choices or changing circumstances in the world or in the course of history.

Christians worship and engage in communion with a God of mercy and justice. And God has created our world with a kind of natural justice that does not allow evil humans or institutions to flourish over the long haul. The self-centered nature of evil itself contains the seeds of its own destruction. It may take time—even decades or centuries—for God's ultimate will of justice to prevail over many human-made evils, but faith and history demonstrate that God's desire for justice is always at work. Oppressive empires fall; hateful institutions implode; sick national leaders lose power; sin self-destructs.

This does not mean that we can quietly wait for God's ultimate justice to work its way in the world or simply give up on justice arriving this side of heaven. The God of mercy and justice is not a disinterested overlord, blandly watching the world like a spectator, but an active, powerful, and empowering agent who always works for good in everything. Therefore, God's ultimate will—and our own gratitude for God's grace—compels us to work and suffer to help make divine mercy and justice living realities in this life. Falling back on God's ultimate will does not take away our responsibility to make choices and take actions that advance God's *intention,* no matter the *circumstance.* God's ultimate will is the prize toward which we strive. It is one chief purpose of the church and part of the mission of every Christian.

Undoubtedly, as we look at the world around us, we know that God's ultimate will for humans and creation has not been realized fully, though we can catch glimpses of the heavenly reality in this life. But through faith, we believe that God's ultimate will can come to pass. Jesus models this belief for us in the prayer he teaches his disciples: "Your will be done, on earth as it is in heaven" (Matt. 6:10).

Weatherhead's powerful clarification of how we can understand and speak about God's will helps us recognize that sometimes we suffer because God loves us enough to give us the freedom to make mistakes. Without this freedom, we would be mere puppets with an erratic and capricious God pulling the strings. God loves us but does not manipulate or coerce us, for neither force nor stage-managing our lives are acts of love. God is certainly powerful enough to halt suffering, but God grants us freedom and human agency out of God's immense love for us.

Weatherhead makes the most vivid differentiation between God's intentional, circumstantial, and ultimate will through the life, death, and resurrection of Jesus. God's *intention* may not have been that Jesus be sent to die, even though we often hear people say that God sent Jesus to die for our sins. If this were the case, why did Jesus travel to Galilee and Judea (and even the taboo area of Samaria), teach and gather disciples, and exhort those around him to follow him? God *intended* for Jesus' followers to repent, believe, and become part of the new reign of God—not to kill him! And this reign, should Jesus have been followed according to God's intention, would have set into motion a revolutionary agent in our world by which God's own attributes, made concrete and real and human, would have banished hatred through love, displaced inequality with justice, and overcome vengeance with mercy. This kind of restoration of creation was God's *intention* through Jesus.

But because of the freedom God grants us and the subsequent evil choices made by humans insensitive to God's intention—as God knew they might be—the *circumstances* arose in which Jesus is forced by evil human choices into the position where he must make a crucial decision: Jesus can either quit proclaiming the truth about human sinfulness and the healing power of love and justice or he must shoulder the consequences of human frailty by allowing himself to be crucified on the cross. Although God may not have intended initially for humankind to reject and crucify the Messiah, the world was clearly free to do so—and its sinfulness made it so inclined. Thus, it *became* God's *circumstantial will* for Jesus to suffer the cross to show the world both the depth of human sinfulness and the breadth of God's *ultimate will* of sacrificial love.

The cross—a seemingly final sign of defeat for God's will in the world—became in itself an expression of God's *ultimate will* accomplished. For God's ultimate will—reconciliation between God and humanity—was accomplished through the life and crucifixion of Jesus. Then, Christ's resurrection secured reconciliation for all time. For in the Resurrection, we see God expressing the ultimate reality of hope within our world and in the world without end. When all seemed like death and suffering on the cross, life and hope and faith and joy exploded in triumphal victory in the Resurrection. For this reason, we herald Easter with trumpets and sing songs of triumph. But this triumph came only by way of God in Christ suffering on a cross.

Therefore, the hope of God's resurrecting power empowers us to endure and to seek wholeness even as we suffer for we know that the crosses we bear will ultimately lead to our resurrections in this life and resurrection with Christ in the life to come. This is the hope of the gospel: Christ has died, Christ is risen, Christ will come again.

This understanding of God's will, explained by Weatherhead during the darkest days of London during WWII, helps us realize very important spiritual truths amid our own strife and struggles. For like the apostle Paul (as translated by Adolf Hansen), when we affirm that "God works for good, in everything," we aren't saying that circumstances won't arise that are difficult or emotionally and spiritually trying. Faith is no insurance policy against tragedy. Yet the words of Paul come to us in the middle of our struggles, representing hope that God's *ultimate will* cannot be and will not be denied. Through faith and trust in God, we may have confidence that even in the darkest night of the soul, even in circumstances that seem far from the love and care God may *intend*, God is still actively "work[ing] for good, in everything." We may not understand how, but we don't necessarily need to. For when we look to the example of Jesus and trust in God, we can remind ourselves that God has not abandoned us and that spiritual growth will result when we *endure* long enough to experience God's resurrecting power. With hope, we may enjoy the privilege of witnessing God's awesome capacity to work for good in ways we could not possibly have anticipated.

Beginnings of Hope

> Therefore, since we are justified by faith, we have peace with God through our Lord Jesus Christ, through whom we have obtained access to this grace in which we stand; and we boast in our hope of sharing the glory of God. And not only that, but we also boast in our sufferings, knowing that suffering produces *endurance*, and endurance produces character, and character produces hope, and hope does not disappoint us, because God's love has been poured into our hearts through the Holy Spirit that has been given to us.
>
> —Romans 5:1-5 (emphasis added)

Paul reminds us that our spiritual pilgrimage from suffering to endurance to character and finally to a hope that "does not disappoint us" may be a long and perilous journey. Yet one of the greatest ways we can grow spiritually is to anchor ourselves in the reality of God's love even during our pain, despair, and struggle. God's love will grant us all the strength and hope we need to face whatever trials we encounter. At the beginning of this path of hope, however, lies suffering. And only during suffering do we find endurance, character, and hope. The lives of countless people stand as witnesses to the fact that our struggles can be redemptive. Although most people engage in struggle unwillingly, they learn through their experience the truths that we read in the Bible.

I remember a young man named Jim when I think about a person who gained immense spiritual growth through suffering. Jim was bright and talented, and his life generally ran smoothly, causing him to be rather spoiled. His parents, like most, wanted the best for their son; they lavished upon him just about everything he needed or wanted to the point that he expected everything to be given to him. Although he would not have said so at the time, he felt entitled to a life with very little struggle and almost no pain. As Jim began considering his plans after his high school graduation, he decided that college would be too much work and got a job working for a contracting firm. His abrupt decision bitterly disappointed his parents, who had long planned and budgeted so that he could attend a university. Some people even wagered that Jim intended to hurt his parents by this decision.

Though Jim decided on a vocation, he lacked a basic direction for his life. He met a young woman, and they soon became engaged. But Jim began to grow disillusioned and bitter that his life as an adult consisted of nothing but financial problems, difficult and often dangerous work, and a future that held few prospects for improvement. He believed he was not getting that to which he was entitled.

Life came crashing down on Jim at a construction site when he fell from an iron beam suspended more than fifty feet above the ground. When Jim awoke several days later, he found himself in the hospital with an injured spine. Doctors told Jim that his injury would leave him a paraplegic. Jim, who had been bitter before the accident, now felt a deep anger, despair, and hopelessness as he was forced into making the long, difficult, and painful adjustment to such a disability. But Jim was equipped with the tools he needed to deal with his new normal, for despite his attempts at taking for granted or hurting those he loved, he had a supportive family, fiancée, and many friends who cared for him. Most importantly, little by little, he came to realize that he had a deep desire to recover even though it would be a painful process.

Jim spent nearly six months in the hospital, enduring several surgeries and engaging in physical therapy that produced agonizingly slow progress. During those months of therapy, Jim had no choice but to remain in his bed, dependent on those around him. He was forced to accept the many things he could not do for himself. His physical powerlessness necessitated that a constant vigil be kept at his bedside. His parents and fiancée, taking turns at the hospital, were with him constantly. During these long hours, Jim conversed with and received encouragement from his family, friends, and loved ones. Many people brought cards and gifts and flowers. People from his church also came by to offer their support and prayers.

Even though many people came by to help, Jim continued to struggle with feelings of bitterness and resentment about his accident. He tried to keep his emotions bottled up inside, but he couldn't. He felt overwhelmed and would cry, angrily punching his fist into his pillow. He sometimes spoke rudely to the nurses and others who tried to help. One day, exasperated by the constancy of the pain and hard work required to cope with his paralysis, Jim lashed out at a visitor from his church. Seething with resentment, he shouted at his visitor, "Don't you dare try to talk to me about God! I don't care. Where was God when I fell? Where is God *now*?"

Jim's friend from church wasn't sure what to say but managed to reply, "I wish I knew why you have to go through this, but I don't. Please know that God is with you and that when you fell, God was right there with you too. And God is with you now, helping you to get stronger. I don't know if that helps. Anyway, it's what I believe."

Unlike scenes in the movies, no fireworks went off; no climactic music accented this experience. Jim was still angry. But this conversation was a turning point for him. He kept on working at his physical therapy and gradually noticed improvement. He never regained the use of his legs, but in time he learned to function proficiently in his battery-powered wheelchair.

The most miraculous part of Jim's healing process was how his attitude toward what had happened to him and about his new life changed. Before the accident and during physical therapy, Jim had a sour personality that tended to repel others. But caring people stayed with him and helped him despite his bitterness. Slowly, through the process of fighting his newfound limitations and receiving the unmerited kindness of others, Jim began to realize that nothing in life could be taken for granted. He grew to appreciate those who cared for him rather than assume someone always would be there to provide for his needs. Even though he recognized the brutal reality that he would never again use his legs, he also realized that he could decide what his attitude toward his circumstances would be. Little things suddenly meant a great deal to him. The cards, visits, and words of encouragement that Jim had initially scorned became important as he learned to appreciate them as gestures of care and love. Jim also realized God was not far off but nearby and that the many people who were helping had been sent by God to offer courage, comfort, and support.

Jim's story is full of pain and despair—but also endurance, spiritual growth, and hope. Jim may not have regained the use of his legs, but he experienced another kind of healing—a deeper fulfillment in life, one he may never have known had he not experienced this tragic accident. God in no way *caused* this accident to force Jim to grow spiritually; instead, Jim's difficult life circumstances presented him with a choice: remain bitter or choose a better path. By his own free volition, Jim chose to work through his pain, to endure, to grow spiritually, and to rely on God for his hope. Jim even found a new confidence in himself through his painful recovery. Not long after Jim and his fiancée married, he launched a small construction firm of his own. Even though life continues to be a struggle, Jim lives it with the fullness of God's hope.

The kinds of spiritual growth to be found through dealing with pain and despair are as many as the people who truly embrace them. All of us must seek out and identify those possibilities for spiritual growth toward which our pain points us. To be sure, God is trying to teach us lessons, but it is up to us to learn.

As we move to the next chapter, let's consider what motivates us to continue in the arduous and sometimes lengthy struggle with pain and despair. Where do we find the strength to continue? Through endurance and hope.

Questions for Reflection

- What are you learning about the importance of discipline as it pertains to helping you grow spiritually amid trials?
- Name one or two (or more) ways your faith is being purified and matured through the refiner's fire.
- How does your new understanding of Romans 8:28 change or reshape how you see God at work in your life?
- In what ways does Weatherhead's explanation of God's *intentional, circumstantial,* and *ultimate will* challenge or confirm your own beliefs about the will of God?

3
Endurance and Hope

Wedged between our experience of discipline and pain, as we begin to notice the first stirrings of hope and spiritual growth resulting from us working through our trials, we may begin to feel as if we can no longer endure our suffering. During this time, when we still have not attained our goals despite having invested great amounts of energy trying to resolve our problems, we again find ourselves confronted with difficult choices: Do we choose faith or doubt, growth or decline, hope or further despair? We feel we have come too far to give up, yet we are too weary from the struggle to endure it for another moment.

During this troublesome phase, we must cultivate a hopeful attitude. For as we engage in our struggles, we may feel tempted to allow our attitude to change. Each of us possesses a personal tolerance for pain and despair, and the circumstances surrounding our struggles vary. Do our experiences, background, and general outlook on life encourage hopefulness? Or do they encourage us to approach struggle with an inward conviction that we should expect the worst? Surrendering to negativity or to a misunderstanding of God's will only feeds the notion that we are helpless and hopeless victims of circumstances beyond our control. Though we sometimes may feel helpless, we needn't be hopeless. Our attitude toward hope, healing, and wholeness greatly influences the speed and scope of the spiritual growth we achieve from the discipline of dealing with pain and despair. And the key ingredients in our approach to difficult times are the mental and spiritual disciplines of *endurance* and *hope*.

Many groups of people throughout history have learned the value of hope while enduring difficult, seemingly impossible life events. The gruesome and dehumanizing persecution of the European Jewish community during Nazi reign reminds us of the human potential for evil. Yet, from the valiant struggle of this people against evil—from the inexpressibly profound pain that has been processed in the years since the Holocaust and continues to be processed by Jews and non-Jews alike—many constructive contributions have been made to our understanding of the resiliency of the human spirit and the importance of endurance and hope.

Among the many moving personal accounts written by survivors of the Nazi death camps is Viktor E. Frankl's

Man's Search for Meaning. While Frankl recounts his experiences at the personal level, he is also remarkably able, from his viewpoint as a trained, professional psychiatrist, to look back and analyze and interpret his own feelings while in the camps. He vividly details the constant threat of extinction that permeated the lives of death camp residents. They found themselves suddenly stripped of personal possessions and individual identity; the stench of flesh-burning furnaces served as an ever-present reminder of death's proximity. The Nazi death machine efficiently pushed the experience of human suffering past any fathomable expectation of mental tolerance or physical survival.

So how did some survive this insult to humanity?

Frankl suggests that the secret to not only the prisoners' survival but also their spiritual growth was to endure with the attitude of hope. Borrowing from the thought of Nietzsche—"He who has a why to live can bear almost any how"—Frankl develops the understanding that even in the worst circumstances imaginable, even when we literally have nothing left, no one or no thing that happens to us can control our own spiritual posture concerning our response to the circumstances in which we find ourselves. Frankl writes the following:

> We who lived in concentration camps can remember the men who walked through the huts comforting others, giving away their last piece of bread. They may have been few in number, but they offer sufficient proof that everything can be taken from a man but one thing: the last of the human

> freedoms—to choose one's attitude in any given set of circumstances, to choose one's own way. . . .
>
> Naturally, only a few people were capable of reaching great spiritual heights. But a few were given the chance to attain human greatness even through their apparent worldly failure and death, an accomplishment which in ordinary circumstances they would never have achieved. To the others of us, the mediocre and the half-hearted, the words of Bismarck could be applied: "Life is like being at the dentist. You always think that the worst is still to come, and yet it is over already." Varying this, we could say that most men in a concentration camp believed that the real opportunities of life had passed. Yet, in reality, there was an opportunity and a challenge. One could make a victory of those experiences, turning life into an inner triumph, or one could ignore the challenge and simply vegetate.[1]

We learn from Frankl that many of those who survived (and many of those who did not) distinguished themselves in their suffering by choosing to live with a hope and human dignity that no one could take away, even in a world turned upside down by unspeakable evil. Their hope made the difference—and their enduring courage.

We cannot hope to find any manner of justification for the suffering of the Holocaust in terms of "valuable lessons" learned from it. It was pure evil in its vilest form. Yet learn from it we can and must; we learn about the ability to hope and endure even in the worst of circumstances. And through hope and endurance, the human spirit is motivated to struggle mightily against agents of pain, despair, and suffering.

As we have seen, pain serves as a signal that we are in physical, emotional, or spiritual danger. Despair, struggle, and the painful discipline (learning) that accompanies them are the ways by which we move through the trials of life to find healing, meaning, and wholeness. And in this crack of time—the time between embracing our pain and despair and our experience of wholeness and spiritual growth—we can choose whether to adopt the attitude of enduring hope. As persons like Frankl show us, hope is not automatically granted to all those who struggle or despair, but it is available to those who are willing to face their despair head on and fight for hope.

Choosing hope again and again—even as despair, struggle, and grief wash over us anew—is the single most important ingredient to blessed endurance. Not making this choice means that our painful experience will not result in much spiritual growth. Worse, we may wallow and become bogged down in despair, which will only leave us feeling more overwhelmed because we will believe that we have tried and failed to deal with our pain, ultimately concluding that trying doesn't work. Then, we will find ourselves in deeper despair than when we started. In the end, we cannot receive the blessings of spiritual growth from our challenges without enduring in hope.

Grief and Hope

For many years, psychiatrists and psychologists have contributed to our understanding of the grief process. Most researchers describe certain stages we pass through in the grieving process. Because we have spent great amounts of time and emotional energy in nurturing relationships that hold immense value, when we suffer a loss we must adjust ourselves to the loss of this relationship by working through the stages of grief and adjustment.

Although we do not advance through the stages in any neatly prescribed order, we can speak of a general progression of the feelings we typically experience while grieving. At first, we feel shocked and may want to deny or avoid our feelings. Shock is a natural coping mechanism built into our bodies and emotions to help us survive trauma. We eventually experience the expression of our emotions, which could manifest itself in physical ailments or a sense of panic. We may feel anger or guilt or a host of other emotions. Finally, usually toward the latter stages of our grief, we slowly begin to feel hope.

Hope is not the only feeling we have as we struggle toward accepting loss. And hope does not automatically appear early in the process to illuminate the path on our journey of grief. Hope comes *gradually*, fading in and out and wrestling with our other feelings; together, these feelings will help us determine our response to pain and despair, separation, and the loneliness we feel. This is why the choice to hope is so important and why it must be made and affirmed time after time.

Although all the emotions we feel as we work through pain and despair are valid—even invaluable—hope is our best friend. Hope motivates us to keep trying when we feel like quitting. Our hope that our pain will one day lessen or subside allows us to cry out to our loved ones once more even when we feel that our rivers of tears have accomplished little. Hope helps us to reach out and openly share our pain with another person even when we feel ashamed, embarrassed, or vulnerable. Hope untangles the web of twisted emotions we have tried to bury deep within. Maintaining hope is a struggle, but it is necessary.

So where do we find hope?

The Emmaus Road Less Traveled: God's Hope Displayed

Like all of us who struggle, suffer, learn, and grow spiritually, the characters portrayed in many biblical stories are forced to search for hope in the midst of despair in their own lives. Such stories (found in both the Hebrew scriptures and the New Testament) that illuminate the meaning of hope are too numerous to summarize here, but a story in the Gospel of Luke offers a good example.

> On that same day two of them were going to a village called Emmaus, about seven miles from Jerusalem, and talking with each other about all

these things that had happened. While they were talking and discussing, Jesus himself came near and went with them, but their eyes were kept from recognizing him. And he said to them, "What are you discussing with each other while you walk along?" They stood still, looking sad. Then one of them, whose name was Cleopas, answered him, "Are you the only stranger in Jerusalem who does not know the things that have taken place there in these days?" He asked them, "What things?" They replied, "The things about Jesus of Nazareth, who was a prophet mighty in deed and word before God and all the people, and how our chief priests and leaders handed him over to be condemned to death and crucified him. *But we had hoped that he was the one to redeem Israel.* Yes, and besides all this, it is now the third day since these things took place. Moreover, some women of our group astounded us. They were at the tomb early this morning, and when they did not find his body there, they came back and told us that they had indeed seen a vision of angels who said that he was alive. Some of those who were with us went to the tomb and found it just as the women had said; but they did not see him." Then he said to them, "Oh, how foolish you are, and how slow of heart to believe all that the prophets have declared! Was it not necessary that the Messiah should suffer these things and then enter into his glory?" Then beginning with Moses

> and all the prophets, he interpreted to them the things about himself in all the scriptures.
>
> As they came near the village to which they were going, he walked ahead as if he were going on. But they urged him strongly, saying, "Stay with us, because it is almost evening and the day is now nearly over." So he went in to stay with them. When he was at the table with them, he took bread, blessed and broke it, and gave it to them. Then their eyes were opened, and they recognized him; and he vanished from their sight. They said to each other, "Were not our hearts burning within us while he was talking to us on the road, while he was opening the scriptures to us?" That same hour they got up and returned to Jerusalem; and they found the eleven and their companions gathered together. They were saying, "The Lord has risen indeed, and he has appeared to Simon!" Then they told what had happened on the road, and how he had been made known to them in the breaking of the bread. (24:13-35, emphasis added)

The disciples also face the temptation to give up hope. Over the course of one week, they have entered Jerusalem with Jesus in triumph only to have their hopes dashed to despair by witnessing their leader's ignominious death upon the cross. They are severely hurt and disillusioned; Jesus, the one in whom they put their hope to deliver their nation and their souls, is dead. The two disciples walking on the road from Jerusalem to Emmaus clearly feel hopeless.

They have heard that Jesus was raised from the dead, but no one has seen him. So they sulk back to Emmaus, grief-stricken and bewildered by their disappointment.

When these disciples complain of their confusion to the stranger—Jesus, whom they fail to recognize—he explains to them the *necessity* of Jesus' suffering and interpreted them "the things about himself in all the scriptures." Yet the disciples do not recognize Jesus or understand who he truly is and what has happened to him until he enters their home and breaks bread with them (Holy Communion). The disciples immediately arise and journey a road less traveled—not the *hopeless* road from Jerusalem to Emmaus but the *hopeful* road from Emmaus back to Jerusalem. Unlike the journey earlier in the day on that same road to Emmaus, this trip back to Jerusalem is filled with a freshly renewed hope and joy from the disciples seeing and experiencing the most wonderful sign God has ever given to our world—the resurrected Christ.

Jesus' death reflects the truth that God is with us in our pain and despair, suffering with us and for us. Similarly, Jesus' resurrection completes a story of hope. For in beholding what theologians call the entire "Christ event"—the life, death, and resurrection of Jesus—we see that pain, despair, and struggle are not the only components of a Christian life. Through the resurrection, we see how God redeems and reclaims suffering, despair, and painful discipline, bringing them to a hopeful and joyous end. Of course, this does not negate the cross or its indescribable pain. Rather, through the resurrection, God moves us through the pain and despair of the cross to a newer, deeper, and hope-filled experience of God's love.

Christians have believed from the beginning of our faith tradition that through this pivotal event in history, God released a mighty force into our world of struggle, pain, and despair. For this reason, the Gospel writers devoted much of their writing to Holy Week, the events leading up to and including Jesus' crucifixion and resurrection. Jesus' resurrection does not just represent hope in an eternal life yet to come; his resurrection also represents the hope that we too will be "resurrected" from our despair and struggle in this earthly life. The resurrection gives us faith that even in our darkest hours, the penetrating rays of hope are never far away and will break through to illuminate our lives and light the way for the rest of our journey.

We may travel the road between Jerusalem and Emmaus many times in our spiritual life. We experience it as a two-lane road of both disillusionment and certainty, despair and hope. But the longer we travel this road, the more thoroughly we will be convinced that the road in either direction is the same. Viewed from one direction we see a journey of sorrow and despair, but viewed from the other direction we may travel in hope.

Jesus' resurrection teaches us that amid our despair, we have the option of taking "the road less traveled": the path from Emmaus back to Jerusalem, the journey of hope. And on that road, we find that our pain and despair are redeemed through Christ's resurrecting power.

The Hope of God's People

As we travel the Jerusalem–Emmaus road with its ever-lurking temptations toward hopelessness and its promise of hope, we can find comfort in other biblical stories that convey human frustrations and struggles. We have seen in the lament psalms the despairing cry of the psalmist who wonders where God has gone and even questions God in allowing such pain and suffering to exist. Yet just as we see the message of pain, despair, and hope in the New Testament writings, we also see hope portrayed in the Psalms and in the history of God's people, the Israelites. Their story, told in the Hebrew scriptures, not only shows us how they question God but also displays the great trust they have in God and their belief that God will deliver them from both their individual and corporate suffering.

This movement from despair to hope often takes place within any one of the lament psalms. For example, in chapter 1 we read from Psalm 13:

> How long, O LORD? Will you forget me forever?
>   How long will you hide your face from me?
> How long must I bear pain in my soul,
>   and have sorrow in my heart all day long? (vv. 1-2)

But the psalm continues in hope:

> I trusted in your steadfast love;
>   my heart shall rejoice in your salvation.
> I will sing to the LORD,

because he has dealt bountifully with me.
(13:5-6)

We also looked at Psalm 38:

My wounds grow foul and fester
because of my foolishness;
I am utterly bowed down and prostrate;
all day long I go around mourning. . . .
I am utterly spent and crushed;
I groan because of the tumult of my heart. (vv. 5-6, 8)

But the psalm continues in hope:

But it is for you, O LORD, that I wait;
it is you, O Lord my God, who will answer. . . .
For I am ready to fall,
and my pain is ever with me. . . .
Do not forsake me, O LORD;
O my God, do not be far from me;
make haste to help me,
O Lord, my salvation. (38:15, 17, 21-22)

Let's also consider Psalm 42:

I say to God, my rock,
"Why have you forgotten me?
Why must I walk about mournfully
because the enemy oppresses me?"
As with a deadly wound in my body,
my adversaries taunt me,

> while they say to me continually,
> "Where is your God?" (vv. 9-10)

And the psalm continues in hope:

> Why are you cast down, O my soul,
> and why are you disquieted within me?
> Hope in God; for I shall again praise him,
> my help and my God. (42:11)

Revealed in these psalms (and in many others) is a dual recognition of pain and distress, along with the strong expression of resolve to place hope in God. The roots of hope run deep in ancient Israel's history and endure to this day. We find the basis for the hope of God's people in one pivotal event: the Exodus of Israelites from Egypt to the Promised Land. A very short time passes between Jesus' crucifixion and his resurrection, but the ancient Hebrew pilgrims wander in the wilderness, longing and hoping for the Promised Land, for forty long years. Before undertaking this miserably long sojourn, God's people spent many years as slaves in Egypt, crying out for God to hear them in their despair. Many who start the journey to the Promised Land never see its completion, including Moses.

All generations of Jews going back 3,000 years have remembered and celebrated God's deliverance of their ancestors (and thereby themselves as well) from bondage. Remembrance of this historical event, the Passover, has provided the primary basis for the belief and hope that pervades Jewish thought—and provides an invaluable basis to Christian thought as well. For Jewish people not only remember and celebrate the deliverance of their ancestors; they also celebrate their present deliverance from bondage and despair. Time after time, we read writers of scripture referring to the Passover as if they are living it in the present. (See Psalm 80:8; Judges 6:7-9; 1 Samuel 10:17-18; Joshua 24:16-17.) Passover is not a simple recalling of the event; it is a living reminder that does not distinguish past from present. During Passover, Jews experience the hope of release from bondage even as they remember the experience of their ancestors and all generations between then and now. Most Christians practice something similar in the "remembrance" of the Last Supper—we don't simply recall that Jesus shares the bread and cup with his disciples in the upper room the night before he dies; we remember that event in communion with one another gathered and the whole company of heaven and the communion of saints. In other words, we share the meal with the disciples, one another, and the entire company of Christian souls who lived, suffered, and died since the first Lord's Supper. This ongoing ritual of acknowledging and dealing with the potential for despair by celebrating deliverance has produced a long and rich Judeo-Christian tradition of hope.

This fundamental and enduring hope that God will deliver God's people allows the prophet Jeremiah to proclaim these words to those who are suffering the separation and despair of exile in a foreign land:

> Only when Babylon's seventy years are completed
> will I visit you, and I will fulfill to you my promise

> and bring you back to this place. For surely I know the plans I have for you, says the LORD, plans for your welfare and not for harm, to give you a future with hope. Then when you call upon me and come and pray to me, I will hear you. When you search for me, you will find me; if you seek me with all your heart, I will let you find me, says the LORD, and I will restore your fortunes and gather you from all the nations and all the places where I have driven you, says the LORD, and I will bring you back to the place from which I sent you into exile. (29:10-14)

That vision of peace includes love, hope, faith, fulfillment, justice, and mercy. But those who suffer find in it what sufferers have found there for many centuries: a vision of hope and meaning for their lives. We are God's people, and despite what feels like evidence to the contrary, God has not forgotten us and will remain faithful.

We can see that the hope God gives to the people of Israel is the same hope God displays in Christ: God is present in the world, actively working through our suffering to offer hope, healing, and deliverance. As we have seen, we cannot expect deliverance *from* suffering, but we can expect hope and deliverance through the pain, despair, and the discipline required to move forward in our spiritual lives.

Endless Hope?

Jesus' words from Psalm 22, which he utters on the cross—"My God, my God, why have you forsaken me?"—also end in hope affirmed by his resurrection. The following is a portion of the remainder of Psalm 22:

> But you, O Lord, do not be far away!
> O my help, come quickly to my aid! . . .
> From you comes my praise in the great congregation;
> my vows I will pay before those who fear him.
> The poor shall eat and be satisfied;
> those who seek him shall praise the Lord.
> May your hearts live forever!
> All the ends of the earth shall remember
> and turn to the Lord;
> and all the families of the nations
> shall worship before him.
> For dominion belongs to the Lord,
> and he rules over the nations.
> To him, indeed, shall all who sleep in the earth bow down;
> before him shall bow all who go down to the dust,
> and I shall live for him.
> Posterity will serve him;
> future generations will be told about the Lord,
> and proclaim his deliverance to a people yet unborn,
> saying that he has done it. (vv. 19, 25-31)

When Jesus quotes Psalm 22, he does so in despair and suffering, bemoaning the tragic end to his life. But the remainder of Psalm 22 does not offer a *hopeless end* but rather an *endless hope*—a hope to be passed from one generation to the next with one fundamental message: God delivers God's people. And through this process of deliverance, God's people grow in spirit, hope, and endurance.

Many people (myself included) have been moved with hope by William Sloane Coffin Jr.'s sermon delivered at Riverside Church in New York (where he was pastor at the time) shortly after the tragic death of his son Alex in a car accident. Coffin concluded his sermon that day in this way:

> And of course I know, even when pain is deep, that God is good. "My God, my God, why hast thou forsaken me?" Yes, but at least, "My God, my God"; and the psalm only begins that way, it doesn't end that way. As the grief that once seemed unbearable begins to turn now to bearable sorrow, the truths in the "right" biblical passages are beginning, once again, to take hold: "Cast thy burden upon the Lord and He shall strengthen thee"; "Weeping may endure for a night, but joy cometh in the morning"; "Lord, by thy favor thou hast made my mountain to stand strong"; "for thou hast delivered my soul from death, mine eyes from tears, and my feet from falling." "In this world ye shall have tribulation, but be of good cheer; I have overcome the world." "The light shines in the darkness, and the darkness has not overcome it."

> And finally I know that when Alex beat me to the grave, the finish line was not Boston Harbor in the middle of the night. If a week ago last Monday a lamp went out, it was because, for him at least, the Dawn had come.
>
> So I shall—so let us all—seek consolation in that love which never dies, and find peace in the dazzling grace that always is.[2]

Our *hope* as we face the difficulties of life is in the never-ending love God has shown the world—love that always surrounds us.

Questions for Reflection

- How do your experiences, background, and general outlook on life encourage hopefulness toward the outcome of your trials? How often do you approach struggle with an inward conviction that your fate cannot be altered?
- What does the life of someone like Viktor E. Frankl teach you about the importance of choosing your response to your trials rather than allowing yourself to feel victimized by them?
- How do the Psalms and Jesus' use of Psalm 22 on the cross encourage you to be honest in your struggles to God? How do the Psalms inspire hope?
- In what ways are you cultivating hope in your life right now?

4

Enduring Hope and Help

In this process of spiritual growth and learning, we begin to recognize the infinite number of ways God offers help in our distress. Among the channels through which we receive God's help, the most direct dimension of assistance comes through prayer. We acknowledged in the first chapter that we sometimes feel alone in our pain and despair since no one else can suffer or grow for us. Let me offer a related truth: No matter how alone we may feel, we are never truly alone in our suffering. For when we feel isolated and abandoned, longing for help from the Source of all growth and hope, God's presence fills our yearning through the discipline of prayer.

However, the kind of help many of us seek in prayer is burdened with misunderstandings. Too often we liken prayer to a presentation of our own personal shopping list to a celestial Santa Claus who will promptly deliver the goods in neatly wrapped packages. And if our wish list does not arrive exactly as we asked and right on our schedule, we nag or complain even more diligently until we either get what we want or give up and tell ourselves God does not care. Obviously, this is not true prayer. But how often are our prayers akin to a spiritual shopping list of what we want and need rather than a time to listen to what God wants and desires of us?

Although petitioning God for our needs is certainly part of hope and prayer, true communion with God is infinitely more meaningful and powerful when we learn to yield to prayer as communication from God, continuously opening ourselves to satisfying and healing experiences of God's hope and help. Prayer is another key ingredient to cultivating Christian endurance.

Writing and reading about the elusive experience of God through prayer is an imprecise exercise. For in speaking of something so mysterious and personal, so holy and communal, words become clumsy tools to communicate the full meaning of a deep relationship with God through prayer. Even so, I will attempt to outline some general guidelines for the kinds of prayer that help us to move from despair to hope. Though a long and rich history of writings on the experience of prayer exists, some aspects of prayer have received more attention in recent years, including the disciplines of silence and solitude, meditation and contemplation, intercessory prayer both individually and corporately, and action in the public sphere for the common good.

In our earlier discussion, we defined *discipline* not as a form of punishment but as an opportunity for growth and learning. Just as athletes must train regularly, we must view prayer as the "gymnasium of the soul." But in this arena, many of us feel uncertain. When it comes to prayer, we assume that we lack the understanding, piety, or spiritual stamina required. The discipline of prayer should not be viewed as a slavish duty to which we must expend every ounce of strength trying to reach an unattainable goal. Rather, we can consider prayer a liberating discipline that opens doors to greater celebration through receiving the balm of God's healing hope and being bathed in enduring grace through God's sustaining presence. Of course, like any other discipline, prayer can be difficult and sometimes painful. But we learn by doing.

In the preface to his book on prayer, Catholic theologian Hans Urs von Balthasar explains the dilemma:

> We would like to pray, but we cannot manage it. Our time of prayer passes leaving us distracted, and since it does not seem to yield any tangible fruit, we are not loath to give it up. From time to time we take up a book of "meditations" which presents us, ready-made, with the contemplation we ought to produce for ourselves. We observe someone else eating, but it does nothing to fill our stomachs. We may read his "meditations", but what we have done is spiritual reading—not

> contemplation. We have seen how someone else has encountered the word of God, we have even profited by his encounter, but all the same it was his and not ours—and we ourselves have achieved nothing. Often because we are too comfortable, which is something that can be overcome. And often out of a fearfulness which robs us of the confidence to take steps on our own.[1]

Humans sometimes feel disinclined to take the medicine that will heal us. And because we avoid the learning and discipline required for prayer, we sometimes find that what holds us back from a richer prayer life is the rigidity of our grip on old habits and ideas about communion with God. We need to let go of our grasp on that which holds us back so that we can move on to greater spiritual heights in prayer.

For this reason, we may find engaging in the discipline of prayer to be difficult during our struggles. This is understandable given the energy-draining nature of hurtful experiences and physical pain, which both demand strenuous effort that even exceeds hard physical labor. In times of pain and suffering, prayer becomes a matter of pleading to God that our suffering and the extreme demands of our energy be alleviated—meaning we may be too busy talking to listen to what God could be saying to us. Of course, God rarely shouts audibly in our ears, but certainly God speaks to us in a "still small voice."

When we make the effort to practice disciplined silence, solitude, meditation, and contemplation, God grants us the possibility for spiritual growth. In regularly practiced silence, we can more ably discern God's whisper. By taking time to read scripture and to meditate or contemplate it in prayer (perhaps using an ancient Christian practice called *lectio divina*), God may grant us new spiritual insights, thoughts, and feelings that can transform our lives. Here—in prayer, silence, meditation, and contemplation—God shows us the way as we journey from despair to hope. These practices nurture Christian endurance.[2]

In our first attempts at contemplative prayer, which may be unfamiliar to many, we may become discouraged because we find that our mind wanders, as von Balthasar observed earlier. We start to pray, but we find ourselves thinking about all sorts of other things. We may start out contemplating and praying but suddenly realize we are replaying recent conversations in our heads or remembering past experiences we either wanted to recall or were trying to forget. My never-ending to-do list plagues me in this kind of prayer.

Rather than castigate ourselves for lack of discipline in retaining spiritual thoughts, why not use these images as part of our prayer? From these random thoughts and images may come significant insights and feelings about ourselves and our relationship with God. In meditation, we may recall meaningful scripture passages or other readings and experiences that have helped us in the past. Advice from friends or family members may bubble up in our thoughts, offering us encouragement and hope. We may even drift into sleep as a gift of renewal amid our exhaustion from dealing with pain. The fresh images and energizing insights found in these times are limitless.

As we enter into a deeper communion with God, we may find that words are increasingly less important as a tool of communication. Sobs and tears, grunts of frustration or sighs of pain or relief become nonverbal prayer. The apostle Paul expresses it this way: "The Spirit helps us in our weakness; for we do not know how to pray as we ought, but that very Spirit intercedes *with sighs too deep for words*. And God, who searches the heart, knows what is the mind of the Spirit, because the Spirit intercedes for the saints according to the will of God" (Rom. 8:26-27, emphasis added). Note that these are the verses that immediately precede Romans 8:28 that we discussed in chapter 2 and may thereby be understood in this context that God's work for our good is an extension of the Spirit's intercession through prayer in our weakness. In our vulnerability as we move beyond despair to hope, prayer allows the Holy Spirit to intercede for us, even when we have no words to express our jumbled thoughts and feelings and can only offer a heavy sigh.

Helpful People

No one can successfully cope with life's despair and struggle, nor its joys and successes, without help from God and other people. Yet many among us apparently believe that living is meant to be a painless and isolated experience. Modern culture (especially American culture) does its best to brainwash us into believing in self-sufficiency and the moral superiority of self-reliance. The image of the "self-made" person permeates our thinking—a person who through hard work and with no help from anyone else makes his or her way to the top of the ladder and attains the respect, wealth, and independence he or she so richly deserves. Such a myth is based on and fosters the illusion that strong people do not need anyone else. But even in our modestly independent acts, we all depend on others. When we go to the grocery to choose and buy our food, do we ever pause to consider how many people were involved in the process of making our food available, farm to aisle? Farmers and farm workers, farm implement makers and repairers, food processing plants and factory workers, truck drivers, butchers, food wholesalers, and grocery personnel are only a few of those involved in the process of growing, preparing, delivering, and selling food to us before we even start to prepare it.

Food production and consumption is but one example of the vast network of interdependencies we rely on every day in America, infrastructures that too many of our impoverished brothers and sisters around the world do not have access to. How silly for us to think that by simply earning a living we have "made it" without the help of others. We are utterly dependent on millions of people that we take for granted daily, beginning with those who are closest to us.

This illusion of independence creeps into our religious thinking as well. We may acknowledge the help of God when things go well (how often we hear athletes thank God for their victories but not for their defeats), but we seldom give others the opportunity to help because we think that we do not—or should not—need it.

We all need to have a strong belief—before God and others—in our worth as individuals. In fact, much of Christian theology is based on God having placed infinite worth on each human being. That belief demands that we value ourselves. But a belief that just "me and Jesus" can face the world is misbegotten, even though this idea is propagated by preachers, the writers of spiritual literature, and even lyrics to popular Christian songs. This belief closes off countless possibilities for receiving the help God offers through others. When we allow ourselves to realize that we are not completely independent and do not need to be—when we realize we need people to love us, appreciate us, and help us—we then allow ourselves to experience spiritual growth in the context of community. We no longer force ourselves to try to face our despair alone. In community with other Christians, we find a hope, help, support, and accountability that are the building blocks of wholeness, healing, and endurance.

Through openness and sharing in community (a small group at church, a Bible study, a choir or music team, a 12-step program), we discover that we are not at all alone in dealing with pain and suffering. We often do not know these things about each other in a typical congregation because we tend not to attend worship and other public events wearing our most painful experiences like brightly colored clothing. We often keep our hurt hidden in public, which is both appropriate in some ways and not in other ways. But when we open our hearts amid a community of supportive people, we find camaraderie and companionship. We find a great source of hope and comfort by sharing our pain and despair with others, whether one-on-one or in a group. And from the soothing balm we enjoy from others' care, we experience even more significant growth and healing. Such contact allows us to discover others who are experiencing similar difficulties so that we may offer our help to them.

The Wounded Healer Stands in the Tragic Gap

Probably the most significant communal spiritual lesson we can reap from our struggles is to learn that help must flow from God through us to others, even when we are facing despair ourselves. For showing others we care is at the very core of what it means to practice Christian love as it has been demonstrated to us through Jesus Christ.

One of the most spiritually gifted writers of his generation was Henri J. M. Nouwen. Among his many insightful books is *The Wounded Healer: Ministry in Contemporary Society*. In describing the difficulties of ministry in our complex world, Nouwen notes that many people suffer because they are "wounded" by a general lack of hope, by loneliness, and by an increasing rootlessness experienced in our highly mobile and restless culture. Nouwen suggests that we can be successful and effective ministers to others only to the degree that we are open to experiencing the wounds of society—that only by truly feeling the hurt of the world can we understand how to help the wounded.[3]

My friend Parker Palmer more recently writes—in much the same spirit as Nouwen—that caregivers and educators must stand in the "tragic gap" in our society between our highest aspirations for civility, human flourishing, and the common good and the dreadful ways too many citizens who live and struggle for basic necessities in the midst of violence, vitriol, and vice. Palmer believes we are called to serve in the tragic gap between our lofty aspirations and the world's horrible realities, especially in vocations like teaching, ministry, social work, medicine, and other helping and healing professions. People who inhabit and labor in this tragic gap as bridges of hope, help, and healing, Parker maintains, require a special brand of courage and need the spiritual practices of supportive community in order to thrive.[4]

Nouwen's idea of the "wounded healer"—as well as Palmer's notion of standing with courage in the "tragic gaps" of our society—are not only extremely helpful among professional clergy and others in the helping professions but also immensely valuable to all who hurt from painful wounds and despair. For the most important feature of the wounded healers or the people standing in the tragic gap is that they turn their attention away from their own despair toward becoming healers of the wounds of people around them. Becoming a wounded healer and standing in the tragic gap both carry tremendous responsibility: We can no longer deny or ignore our own pain and despair for this denial robs us of our vital ability to empathize with our brothers and sisters who suffer around us. By refusing to suffer our hurt and despair alone, we learn that many other wounded healers stand with us in many kinds of tragic gaps.

Living as a wounded healer or standing in the tragic gap not only increases our responsibility to help heal or lighten the burdens of others but also mysteriously lessens our own load. So becoming a wounded healer, paradoxically, is a means through which we receive God's helpful healing for our own wounds by reaching out to help God heal others. Until we break away from a preoccupation with our own despair by reaching out from it to help others, we will not fully experience the richest dimensions and meaning of spiritual growth. Nestled in community is where we find strength for God's endurance. This type of community is found only in that degree to which we are willing to move beyond ourselves to consider the needs of others. As we have seen, our sense of community may be found partly in a church group, but all of us can find other opportunities to share with others. Ultimately, when we participate in helping others in community, we will receive support for our own spiritual growth.

Being a wounded healer or standing in the tragic gap are not difficult concepts to understand—yet they are tremendously difficult to achieve and sustain. Being a wounded healer may be as simple as nodding our head in affirmation when a friend shares a burden or as difficult as facing the long, lingering death of a much-loved family member or friend. It may mean the patient endurance of having coffee every week for a year or even two with a friend who has lost a spouse or child to death. Standing in the tragic gap may mean volunteering in a food ministry located in an urban food desert, becoming a Big Sister or Big Brother, tutoring in an impoverished neighborhood, or standing alongside those who are fighting for their rights.

Through experiencing this paradoxical relationship between despair and hope, wounds and healing, community and help, we find the deepest meaning of *blessed endurance*: allowing ourselves and others to feel and experience the seemingly opposite emotions that we find at the very core of life in God through Christ. The *agony* of Jesus on the cross and the *joy* of the resurrected Christ—*taken together*—are our model of Christlike endurance. Here despair and hope are merged seamlessly in such a way that it no longer matters *why we* suffer, for our attention is focused on probing the meaning of participating in the life of a suffering God in service of others in a suffering world in need of healing, what the Jewish tradition calls *tikkun olam* (the repair or healing of the world) and what Christians call the kingdom (or reign) of God.

Few people obtain such spiritual heights. Most of us look up to them as one admires the lofty achievements of a mountain climber from the safe, level ground below. Yet when we meet one who has scaled the highest spiritual peaks, we also usually find that they are among those who have suffered the most pain and despair. These people are like Moses, who led his people from bondage and struggled up the mountain to stand in the very presence of God. This experience transformed Moses; he had lived for a moment or two in divine splendor and was forever changed. One such Moses was a dear friend named Mance Gilliam.

Mance

Mance Gilliam was the youngest of twelve brothers and sisters born into a North Carolina African American sharecropper's family during the earliest part of the twentieth century. His mother dreamed that one of her children someday would attend college. Although the Gilliam family had little money, they saved what they had and pooled available financial resources, funneling cash from the oldest child down so that the youngest member might receive the education that had long been their mother's dream. Through his family's love and labor and much hard work on his own, Mance successfully graduated from Livingstone College in Salisbury, North Carolina, and almost immediately began working for the North Carolina Mutual Insurance Company, which was one of the largest African American owned businesses in the nation. This company provided the only insurance option available to many African American citizens of its region at that time. In the years and decades to come, Mance advanced to the position of vice president, supervising the company's field insurance agents. Mance's career was highly successful and rewarding.

But Mance did not reserve his skills and talents for business use only. He also served as a leader in his local church as well as in his denomination, the African Methodist Episcopal Church, Zion. He was elected a delegate to every General Conference of his denomination between 1948 and 1976. From his extensive travels and influence throughout the South, Mance also attained a position from which he assisted struggling historic black colleges so that they could remain open during the financially challenging years of the Great Depression and following WWII. His work with these institutions of higher learning, one of which he felt privileged to have attended, was perhaps his proudest achievement.

When I first met Mance, he had been retired for about ten years and was in his late seventies. He was working as a volunteer fundraiser for a senior citizens' agency serving mostly low-income residents in Durham, North Carolina. The people who lived in the senior housing project attached to the agency were principally retired domestic workers, sharecroppers, and day laborers, many of whom lived on minimum Social Security income and unsupplemented Medicare benefits. Mance greeted each person every day as he came to work with a spring in his step and an unmistakable vibrancy in his smile. He volunteered an average of thirty to forty hours per week during his retirement. No one who witnessed his energy and attitude would have believed that he was older than many of the residents, but most of them had lived difficult, hardscrabble lives.

Mance took me under his wing as a young pastoral intern at this agency. I have never known why. His kindness was unexpected (to me) but typical (of him). He would take me aside quietly, allow me to ask questions, listen to me patiently, and help me discern my calling. I now understand that his mentorship helped him remain youthful in spirit.

During long talks over lunch, Mance shared the struggles of his life with me. His wisdom had grown out of the profound mixture of challenge and willpower, despair and hope, scarcity and sufficiency he had experienced. He inspired me by communicating not only fascinating events but also perceptive spiritual interpretations of his experiences. In all his struggles with racism, including communities trying their best to bankrupt the financially fragile black colleges he worked with, Mance saw a larger spiritual battle being waged between racial prejudice and divine justice. In his work for the insurance company, he saw God's care for oppressed people by providing valuable financial protection to those who couldn't find such security elsewhere. And in his work with senior citizens, Mance saw the opportunity to serve those who had not been as fortunate as he, devoting long hours and extensive energy to raising funds and building relationships. For Mance, these efforts were not woeful duty; rather, they were spontaneous acts of gratitude for the people he believed had helped him all his life. He was thankful and returned these blessings into help for others in need.

Mance had seen and faced more pain, conflict, and despair than I could ever imagine. Yet for him, each encounter was essentially a *spiritual* struggle. He made no separation between the sacred and the secular. His insurance career, church outreach, work with historic black colleges, and volunteering were all the same: They were service to God, and they represented a commitment to blessed endurance. It was his ability to face—even seek out—such experiences that made Mance one of the most remarkable people I have ever known.

As a young and inexperienced student preparing for the ministry, I began to complain to Mance about some of the sacrifices the church expects professional ministers to make. Mance chuckled and gave me some advice I will never forget. "Even though I wasn't a preacher, I once wrestled with that devil too," Mance replied. "One time, I remember, there was a Sunday morning when I was thinking hard about dumping everything I was doing. I was weary from fighting all that mess out there," he said with a sweeping gesture, seeming to refer to the whole world of strife. "I was working with those colleges in Birmingham and Atlanta that were having a hard time and were calling on me. Oh, it was chaos! Everybody fussing and carrying on, wringing their hands over this and that, saying, 'What are we going to do? What are we going to do?' I felt like I couldn't take it anymore, and I'll tell you I was wrestling with the temptation to give up the fight. Called for too much sacrifice. Too hard! It had gotten so bad I didn't even feel like going to church one morning, and I hadn't missed a Sunday in *years*!" Then Mance leaned over the table, his piercing green eyes widening with intensity as he fixed his gaze squarely on me. "But I went to church that Sunday morning anyway.

"And do you know what the preacher talked about?" Mance continued. "He talked about Saint Paul telling Titus to stay in Crete. You know that story—in Paul's letter to young Titus, he told him to stay in Crete and to preach the Word. Now Titus didn't *want* to stay there. Crete was an awful place—full of false preachers, everybody wrangling amongst themselves. I've been there on a Holy Land tour. Rocky, barren kind of a place. Sort of reminded me of what I was going through. But Paul said to Titus,"—and here Mance spoke slowly, lowering his voice to a whisper as he pointed at me and leaned even closer—"Stay in Crete, Titus. Stay in Crete."

Then, Mance sat back, suddenly relaxed, leaning back on legs of his chair with his thumbs tucked in behind his belt. He remained silent for a little while, looking at me with a sly smile. Finally, he said, "The preacher was talking right to me, you see. It was like God reaching down, grabbing me by the collar, and saying to me even in the middle of all that mess I was in, 'Mance, stay in Crete; stay in Birmingham; stay in Atlanta; keep helping your people.' When I heard those words that Sunday morning, I knew I just couldn't give up. So we kept on fighting, and before long we had convinced those old Bull Connor boys in Birmingham to help us keep that school open."

Mance's fiery intensity reappeared as he again pointed and leaned forward to look me directly in the eye: "Son, what I'm saying to you is stay in Crete. Stay in Crete! I know it's a mess and painful and a struggle in constant battle with despair. But stay in Crete!" Mance's words have remained with me to this day. I once heard someone say, "If you haven't seen God in the eyes of another person, you haven't seen God!" That day, I couldn't help but see God in the eyes of Mance Gilliam.

Months later, Mance's wife called me out of the blue to say that he had been hospitalized. When I went to see him, Mance was unconscious. After only a few more days, he died. Though I felt his death had been sudden, Mance's wife later shared that Mance had been terminally ill with prostate cancer for several years. He had chosen to tell this news only to a few close friends and church members because he wanted to continue working and helping people and not have them fuss over him—a wounded healer standing in the tragic gap to the very end.

Mance's words remind me of how he lived his entire life. Even while bearing the wounds and battle scars left from a life full of strife—when others might have admitted defeat or told themselves they had done their part—Mance spent his last days helping others move from despair to hope. He worked for the comfort of others even in his own great discomfort. Mance embraced the burden and the joy of finding that despair and hope journey together in a life of faith. He demonstrated that nothing outlasts the influence of spiritual growth gained through struggle, pain, discipline, and despair that lead to joy, hope, faith, love, and trust in God. He lived *blessed endurance.*

Questions for Reflection

- How often are your prayers akin to a spiritual shopping list of what you want and need rather than pausing to listen to what God wants and needs of you?
- Cultivate a contemplative prayer practice. For example, read a short passage of scripture—or even some lines from this book that you want to explore deeper—and let your mind relax and focus only on the passage for fifteen minutes. Listen to what God may be saying to you now about this passage. After practicing this method several times, ask yourself what was different about this "listening" prayer technique from a technique that focuses on "talking" to God.
- How can you be a wounded healer or stand in a tragic gap for others? Think of concrete examples, and give them a try! Reflect on the difference your actions can have on your own life and on the lives of others.
- Where is Crete for you? What does it mean for you to stay there?

(UNEXPECTED) EPILOGUE

I had planned and written a very different epilogue to close this book. But the very week I was putting the finishing touches on the manuscript, I found out some troubling medical news. Out of the blue, ER doctors accidentally discovered that I have cancer, though I did not exhibit any symptoms. The cancer was already quite advanced though highly treatable; it's incurable but not terminal. Needless to say, that week was one the fiercest life-changing periods of my entire life.

When sharing this news with my editor, Joanna Bradley, she said, "I'm so sorry you must now live out the blessed endurance you have written about." Her words stuck with me through a whirlwind week of diagnostic testing, surgery, medical appointments, and the beginning of chemotherapy. Later, she and I discovered that we both had considered the possibility that I should relate this news to you, the reader, even as I am just beginning what looks to be a long, bumpy, and uncertain journey.

I share my story not in the spirit of seeking pity or as a play for your sympathy; I am defined by neither disease nor disaster. I am a child of God first and foremost, above all circumstances. Instead, I share this news to express my solidarity with those who face trials and to show that I—the author of a book on pain and despair—am not immune from the struggles this book describes. Many times in my life, I have traveled a journey of suffering, surrounded by the support of my family, friends, coworkers, fellow church members, as well as the communion of saints, that "great cloud of witnesses" praying for and with me. I want to share the passage from Hebrews that mentions the "cloud of witnesses" because it has shaped my life and sums up my thoughts:

> Therefore, since we are surrounded by so great a cloud of witnesses, let us also lay aside every weight and the sin that clings so closely, and let us run with perseverance the race that is set before us, looking to Jesus the pioneer and perfecter of our faith, who for the sake of the joy that was set before him endured the cross, disregarding its shame, and has taken his seat at the right hand of the throne of God. Consider him who endured such hostility against himself from sinners, so that you may not grow weary or lose heart. (12:1-3)

In the end, this book may have been written for the benefit of my own soul as much as yours.

Now it is time for me to learn again how to live into the words I have written. I must rely on the honesty and promises of the scriptures I have quoted, look to Jesus on the cross as God's expression of suffering love and oneness with me and all who are in pain or despair, avail myself of the Christian faith's treasury of wisdom that has been passed down for generations about how to deal with life's trials, master my pride that falsely tells me I can travel this treacherous path alone without guides or assistance, embrace humility in admitting my need to accept help in this time of affliction (and at all times), and, above all, practice the undervalued virtue of Christian *endurance*—the power that overflows from the hope of the Resurrection, that overcomes the grip of disease, trauma, pain, despair, and grief in this life and that has ultimately conquered death itself.

In looking back over a final edit of my own words during the last troubling week, I am struck that I still believe every word. This is not to say I am not afraid about what this struggle means for me and my family. I wonder *why* this is happening to me; I feel apprehensive about the effectiveness of treatments and my long-term prognosis. I even foresee moments when I will cry out to God in anguish. But above all, I will try to cultivate hope and trust that God has not abandoned me, that God is *here* in my every *now*.

In my daily prayer guide today, I encountered another passage from Paul's letter to the church in Rome: "Let love be sincere; hate what is evil, hold on to what is good; love one another with mutual affection; anticipate one another in showing honor. Do not grow slack in zeal, be fervent in spirit, serve the Lord. *Rejoice in hope, endure in affliction, persevere in prayer"* (Rom. 12:9-12, NABRE, emphasis added).

In this spirit, I offer a prayer for myself and for you—a prayer of hope, endurance, and perseverance.

Thy ultimate will be done, O God, even in circumstances you did not intend. May your power and grace fall upon all who suffer so that we may grow in endurance, remembering Christ's example so that we may "not grow weary or lose heart" in the journey of moving from despair to hope. Give us strength, we pray, to "rejoice in hope, endure in affliction, persevere in prayer." Amen.

Indianapolis, Indiana
August 12, 2017

NOTES

Chapter 2: Moving toward Spiritual Growth

1. Martin E. Marty, *A Cry of Absence: Reflections for the Winter of the Heart* (San Francisco: Harper & Row, 1983), 3.
2. Adolf Hansen, *Three Simple Truths: Experiencing Them in our Lives* (Portland, OR, Inkwater Press, 2014), 27–50. See Chapter 2: "God Works for Good, In Everything."
3. Leslie D. Weatherhead's *The Will of God* was originally published in London in 1944 during the war. It immediately became immensely popular and has remained in print for almost seventy-five years, sold more than a million copies worldwide, and has been published in numerous editions over the decades. As pastor of London's well-known City Temple (one of England largest Methodist congregations, which after its destruction during the war was rebuilt and rededicated in 1954) and author of at least fifty-four books, Weatherhead is the subject of several biographies. For a more recent edition of this book, see Leslie D. Weatherhead, *The Will of God.* rev. ed. (Nashville, TN: Abingdon Press, 1999).

Chapter 3: Endurance and Hope

1. Like Leslie D. Weatherhead's *The Will of God*, Viktor E. Frankl's *Man's Search for Meaning* has been published in many editions since it first appeared in 1946. See Viktor E. Frankl, *Man's Search for Meaning*, trans. Ilse Lasch (Boston: Beacon Press), 65, 72.
2. William Sloane Coffin Jr., "Alex's Death," in *This Incomplete One: Words Occasioned by the Death of a Young Person*, ed. Michael D. Bush. (Grand Rapids, MI: William B. Eerdmans, 2006), 60.

Chapter 4: Enduring Hope and Help

1. Hans Urs von Balthasar, *Prayer*, trans. Graham Harrison (San Francisco: Ignatius Press, 1986), 7.
2. For those who wish to learn more about contemplative prayer, I highly recommend one in a series of books written by my spiritual director, Sr. Mary Margaret "Meg" Funk. See Mary Margaret Funk, *Lectio Matters: Before the Burning Bush*, The Matters Series (Collegeville, MN: Liturgical Press, 2013). I also highly recommend the other books in the five-volume The Matters Series, which includes *Thoughts Matter: Discovering the Spiritual Journey; Tools Matter: Beginning the Spiritual Journey; Discernment Matters: Listening with the Ear of the Heart; and Humility Matters: Toward Purity of Heart.*
3. Henri J. M. Nouwen, *The Wounded Healer: Ministry in Contemporary Society* (New York: Image Books, 1979).
4. Parker J. Palmer, *Healing the Heart of Democracy: The Courage to Create a Politics Worthy of the Human Spirit* (San Francisco: Jossey-Bass, 2014). The Center for Courage & Renewal, an organization cofounded by Parker

Palmer and Rick and Marcy Jackson that strives to make Palmer's vision for personal and societal renewal a living reality in our world, has on its website a short, free video of Palmer explaining his concept of the tragic gap. See http://www.couragerenewal.org/the-tragic-gap/.

CPSIA information can be obtained
at www.ICGtesting.com
Printed in the USA
LVOW03s1149081217
559081LV00010B/76/P